and they discovered to their surprise that Ives was way ahead of them.

The story of Charles Ives is the story of a man who made music not for his own time, but for the people who would come after him. It is the story of genius.

Helen R. Sive's first experience with the music of Charles Ives came in a high school choir, singing two of the composer's small masterpieces—"Serenity" and "Psalm 67." This lead her to an appreciation of America's great composer that many have shared with equal enthusiasm.

A New Yorker, Ms. Sive received her B.A. from Oberlin College. She is presently studying towards a Master's degree in music at Columbia University.

MUSIC'S CONNECTICUT YANKEE

*An Introduction
to the Life and Music
of Charles Ives*

Helen R. Sive

MUSIC'S CONNECTICUT YANKEE

An Introduction to the Life and Music of Charles Ives

ILLUSTRATED WITH PHOTOGRAPHS

Atheneum · 1977 · New York

Library of Congress Cataloging in Publication Data

Sive, Helen R
Music's Connecticut Yankee:
An introduction to the life and music
of Charles Ives

SUMMARY: Follows the life and discusses the music
of the insurance executive who composed in his spare time
music of such originality and variety that
he ranks today as one of this country's greatest
and most thoroughly American composers.
Bibliography: p. 131.
Includes index.
1. Ives, Charles Edward, 1874-1954.   [1. Ives,
Charles Edward, 1874-1954.   2. Composers]   I. Title.
ML3930.I94S6   780'.92'4 [B] [92]   76-25000
ISBN 0-689-30561-3

Contents

Introduction   xi

1. An Old New England Family and Its Musical
   Sons   3
2. George and Charles Ives: First Experiments
   with Music   16
3. Yale Years   23
4. Early Years in New York   36
5. New Musical Discoveries, The Life Insurance
   Business and Harmony   48
6. Ives in His Prime   65
7. The Fourth Symphony   81
8. Ives's Retirement from Music: The Beginnings
   of an Audience   92
9. New Friends   106
10. A Great American Composer   115

   Afterword   129
   Suggestions for Further Reading   131
   Summary of the Principal Works of Charles
      Ives with Some Suggested Recordings   133
   Index   137

Acknowledgements

I would like to thank John Kirkpatrick for his careful reading and helpful suggestions when this book was in earlier stages; Vivian Perlis for help in securing illustrations; and Emily Granrud for countless valuable criticisms and suggestions.

Introduction

Now that it is more than one hundred years since Charles
Ives was born, many people would say that he was probably the best thing that ever happened to American
music. His ideas and his music have brought freshness
to our musical life over the past thirty-five years, and
will continue to do so for many more.

Ives was one of those musical revolutionaries who
seems to have been thrust into the world at just the time
he was most needed. The American musical scene was
perfectly set up for his entry. Before Ives was born,
there was hardly anything one could have called a genuine tradition of American music. There was a great
wealth of folk music in the nation, fine enough to com-
pare with that of any country, but somehow the idea of
genuine American music had not yet spread into the
area of classical—or art—music.

There were reasons for this. One was that in the
nineteenth century many Americans had the idea that
the only way to train musicians properly was to ship

them off to Europe and have them absorb all the great artistic traditions of Germany, France, Italy and other countries. The unfortunate result of this practice is obvious to us now—the Americans came home to write European music, which did little to further the cause of music in their homeland.

Ives was the first significant American composer to see the richness of his own culture and resolve to feed his imagination on it, without help from the Europeans. One way he did this was by using a great deal of native American music in his works. This was not an unusual practice. Many composers—Beethoven, Grieg, Dvorak, Mahler and others—had also found inspiration in their native music and had incorporated it into their compositions. So Ives was really only doing what should have been natural for an American composer to do—write American music.

Ives not only freed American music from European binds; he also freed music from its own historical binds. Like other great twentieth century composers, he showed the world that music can be something more than beautiful sounds. Ives has shown that music can be a mirror to our lives—it can express the ways each person sees the world around him.

In order to attain this, Ives saw that music had to

be freer than it had been in the centuries before our own. It had to forget about rules—to use any sounds it wanted, and to organize these sounds in any way that gave them significance. Like Debussy, Mahler, Schoenberg and Stravinsky, Ives saw that in order for music to be free, a composer had to be completely free in deciding how it should be written. Ives expressed this view, rather humorously, in the "Postface" to his collection *114 Songs.*

Some of the songs in this book, particularly among the later ones, cannot be sung,* and if they could, perhaps might prefer, if they had a say, to remain as they are. . . . An excuse . . . for their existence which suggests itself at this point is that a song has a few rights, the same as other ordinary citizens. If it feels like walking along the left-hand side of the street, passing the door of physiology or sitting on the curb, why not let it? If it feels like kicking over an ash can, or a poet's castle, or the prosodic law, will you stop it? If it wants to beat around in the valley, to throw stones up the pyramids, or to sleep in the park, should it not have some immunity from a Nemesis, a Rameses, or a

* (by celebrated opera singers)

policeman? Should it not have a chance to sing to itself, if it can sing?—to enjoy itself without making a bow, if it can't make a bow?—to swim around in any ocean, if it can swim, without having to swallow "hook and bait," or being sunk by an operatic greyhound? If it happens to feel like trying to fly where humans cannot fly, to sing what cannot be sung, to walk in a cave on all fours, or to tighten up its girth in blind hope and faith and try to scale mountains that are not, who shall stop it?

> —In short, must a song
> always be a song!

Exploring Ives's life helps us to understand how he came to have such revolutionary ideas about music.

MUSIC'S CONNECTICUT YANKEE

---

*An Introduction
to the Life and Music
of Charles Ives*

1

An
Old New England Family
and Its Musical Sons

Charles Ives grew up in the small town of Danbury, Connecticut, which lies among the gently rolling hills of Fairfield County, about forty miles north of New York City. In the years after the Civil War, when the town was becoming one of the most important centers of industry and business in the state, the Ives family had acquired a position of influence there and in the surrounding area.

In 1874, the year of Charlie's birth, one of the town's leading citizens was George Ives, Charlie's father. The family had always been proud of its independent thinkers, men who had been active in business, law and politics, but George Ives had added a new dimension to the family history. Not only was he a bandmaster, a choral conductor and an accomplished performer, he was one of the most original musicians of the nineteenth century.

Musical talent was not much in evidence in the family before George Ives was born, though the family history was a long one. It was just fifteen years after the Plymouth Colony in Massachusetts was first settled that the first Ives came to Connecticut. This was William Ives, who sailed from England on the "Truelove" and helped eventually to found New Haven, which is now the largest city in the state. William's family expanded rapidly, and the name Ives became associated with successful bankers, lawyers and businessmen. But there were no musicians.

Finally, after two hundred years, a musical talent appeared in the person of Elam Ives, a well-known music educator and editor in the early part of the nineteenth century. Years later Charles Ives set to music one of the poems he found in Elam Ives's *Musical Spelling Book*, which was published in 1846.

George Ives was the second member of the family to choose music as a profession. His parents discovered his extraordinary gift for music when he was just a young boy and were wise enough to send him to New York City to obtain a thorough education in the subject. George eagerly attended the classes in music until the year 1862. The country being then in the midst of the Civil War, he temporarily gave up school, for he had decided to listen to the advice of his father's cousin, Colonel Nelson White. White had suggested that George put his musical talents to more practical use and organize an army band. Within a short time George found himself the leader of the First Connecticut Heavy Artillery Band.

At the age of seventeen George had the distinction of being the youngest bandmaster in the Union Army. There were numerous people who even said that his band was the army's finest. A legendary story tells about the time President Abraham Lincoln and General Ulysses S. Grant had the pleasure of listening together to the band. The president remarked, "That's a good band!" and his general replied, "It's the best band in the army, they tell me, but you couldn't prove it by me. I only know two tunes. One is 'Yankee Doodle' and the other isn't." Suffice it to say, the general was an inexperienced listener; but such people never bothered George Ives very much. In fact, he often found their frank observations refreshing and valuable.

Charles Ives later explained why his father's band had pleased the president and the general so much:

> Father also had a gift for playing. He'd take a familiar piece and play it to make it mean more than something just usual. . . . The things he

played then (during the war) were mostly the things that most bands played, but he put something in them that most band leaders didn't—ask Mr. Lincoln or Mr. Grant!

After the war ended, George went back to New York to resume his studies; and in 1868 he returned to Danbury and began his professional career. As a band leader in Danbury, he found his experience with the army to be quite valuable. Before long he was conducting not only three bands in Danbury, but the bands in the nearby towns of Bethel, Brewster and New Milford as well. In most everyone's opinion, he was quite successful.

It was New Year's Day in 1874 when George Ives married Mary Elizabeth Parmalee, the daughter of a local farmer from Bethel. There was a musical bent in her family, too, for her mother was a choir singer of some importance in the area. In October of the same year, George and Mary's first child, Charles Edward, was born. Two years later Charles had a baby brother— Joseph Moss, or "Mossie," as he later came to be called.

The childhoods of Charlie and Mossie Ives were happy ones. This was due in part to the pleasant New England town in which they lived. They had few social problems as they were growing up, for everyone knew that they came from one of the busiest, most respectable families in Danbury. Their relatives were numerous and came often to the Ives house to visit. Charlie and Mossie had plenty of cousins to play with, especially during the summers when the whole family went to Westbrook, Connecticut.

The old Ives house, where both Charlie and Mossie were born, sat right on Main Street amid towering elm trees. This allowed the boys to take in all the interesting events of the town. Like other small nineteenth century New England towns, Danbury had its share of parades, fairs, town meetings and other colorful activities.

Charlie and Mossie spent a good deal of time, when not in school, working on various projects. One of their favorites was the management of their own miniature grocery store (Ives Bros. Grocery), a game that was carried out with great seriousness. The store was housed in the woodshed in back of their grandmother's home. Complete with their own printed stationery and fairly exact bookkeeping, the whole enterprise was quite thorough and seemed to show that the two boys had inherited the family "business sense."

In addition, Mossie seemed to lean toward the Ives family tradition of interest in public affairs, and Charlie, like his father, showed a remarkable gift for music. George was no doubt pleased with this. He proudly told

George Edward Ives as a bandmaster, around 1892. PHOTO-
GRAPH COURTESY JOHN HERRICK JACKSON MUSIC LIBRARY, YALE
UNIVERSITY.

his friends and relatives of his son's first musical accomplishment—learning how to play the drums. These lessons were given on an old washtub by the local barber, Schleier, in his barbershop. He had played the drums in George Ives's Civil War Army band. Within a short while, Charlie was proudly playing the snare drum in his father's band.

But Charlie's father was his first real music teacher, and the one who ultimately had the greatest influence on him. From the earliest sign of Charlie's musical talent and interest, George Ives devoted himself to teaching his son all the music the young boy could possibly absorb. At first the instruction was mainly practical, with lessons in playing the piano, violin and cornet, one of George Ives's favorite instruments. After a while there came lessons in music theory, which included all the fundamentals of harmony and counterpoint, the two aspects of musical theory most important to composers. Charlie picked up everything with relative ease, much to the satisfaction of his father and mother.

George Ives had special ideas about teaching that set him apart from other music teachers. Unlike most teachers, who do not encourage creativity in their students, George Ives always insisted that his son and his other students use the music they learned imaginatively. To merely know how music was made was not enough.

9

It was also important to make it in one's own way. The value of this method of teaching in Ives's later career was enormous.

George Ives's teaching efforts were not forgotten, by his son or his other students. For years he was the center of musical life in Danbury. The people he taught —the members of his bands, and many of the children of the town—remembered all their lives the music he helped them understand. He taught them to love music of all kinds—from simple hymn tunes sung at camp meeting services to Schubert songs and Beethoven symphonies.

George Ives's influence extended beyond music, too. Both Mossie and Charlie were impressed with their father's interest in town affairs. George obviously cared deeply about the welfare of the town. He also worked for the Danbury Bank for a time. This led Mossie, who also learned music from his father but who was not as gifted as his brother, to become interested in the town's history and politics. Later he started a school newspaper with some friends, which made his father as proud as Charlie's musical achievements did.

All who knew Charles Ives in his later life were aware of his deep respect for his father's views and abilities, as a person, as a musician and as a teacher. One passage from Ives's recently published *Memos* explains these feelings clearly:

He had a belief that everyone was born with at least one germ of musical talent, and that an early application of great music . . . would help it grow. He started all the children of the family —and most of the children of the town for that matter—on Bach and Stephen Foster . . . I feel that, if I have done anything that is good in music, I owe it almost entirely to him and his influence.

2

George and Charles Ives: First Experiments with Music

Most important in Charlie's early musical background was his father's constant experiments with music. Perhaps it was his firm New England upbringing that had taught him the value of a challenge, but wherever it came from, George Ives was always eager to create challenges for himself and his students. The most important of his musical challenges his son later nicknamed "ear-stretching." It meant trying to produce new and unusual sounds and knowing exactly how they were made. Most ear-stretching experiments were astoundingly difficult, especially for a young boy, but through daily practice, by the age of ten or eleven Charlie was able to master such small feats as being able to sing the tune "Swanee River" in the key of E flat major while playing it in C major on the piano. Both father and son

spent many fascinating hours in these experiments, be-
lieving not only in their musical value but feeling that
as intellectual challenges they would help to build strong
character.

George Ives's penchant for musical challenges came
largely from his intense interest in the whole world of
sound. This world embraced not only formal music, but
all the sounds produced by nature and by man. He was
particularly interested in sound "accidents," the kinds
of sounds produced by people singing different tunes
simultaneously, or by the activities and conversations
one hears walking down the street. These sound "hap-
penings" also fascinated his son, who studied them and
later worked them into his compositions.

George Ives's interest in the world of sound led him
into all kinds of unusual experiments, some of which
were quite advanced for a man of the nineteenth century.
Music at that time was still ruled primarily by the sys-
tem that had been used by Mozart, Haydn, Beethoven
and other composers of the classical period. Even the
well-known composers of George Ives's day, among
them Brahms, Wagner, Berlioz and Liszt, had not really
broken away from the old systems, even though all were
great musical innovators. American composers of the
time, like Edward Macdowell, were more tied down than
their European contemporaries to the basic forms and

styles of the eighteenth and early nineteenth centuries. But George Ives was a revolutionary. He respected old ideas, but he was more than open to new ones.

One of George Ives's favorite preoccupations was the study of "quarter tones." Quarter tones can be briefly described as tones in between the half tones that form the chromatic scale. An easier way to understand this is to imagine a piano with extra keys added between the already-present keys.

These notes were difficult to sing and to produce on instruments. George Ives spent many of his spare hours teaching himself and his students how to sing quarter tones, and he even tried to build a quarter tone instrument. Charles Ives remembered his father's curiosity clearly:

One afternoon, in a pouring thunderstorm, we saw him standing without hat or coat in the back garden; the church bell next door was ringing. He would rush into the house to the piano, and then back again. "I've heard a chord I've never heard before—it comes over and over, but I can't seem to catch it." He stayed up most of the night trying to find it on the piano. It was soon after this that he started his quarter-tone machine.

14

The quarter-tone machine was built with twenty-four violin strings stretched across a clothes press. It must have created a somewhat bizarre sight for George Ives's friends, musicians and non-musicians alike. In fact, they probably looked at most of Ives's strange musical experiments as the work of an eccentric, as Charles Ives later suggested:

> Father had a kind of natural interest in sounds of every kind, everywhere, known or unknown, measured "as such" or not, and this led him into positions or situations . . . that made some of the townspeople call him a crank whenever he appeared in public with some of his contraptions.

However, the opinions and comments of the townspeople never really bothered George Ives, and he stuck to his own ideas in spite of public opinion. Both he and his son believed fervently in the importance of pursuing one's own ideas, no matter what the opinion of others might be. There was a strong bond between their belief in individuality and in Ralph Waldo Emerson's idea of self-reliance. In his essay "Self Reliance" Emerson wrote that only those men who were not swayed by public opinion could achieve real virtue. He believed that each man had a responsibility to discover for himself what was good, and that other people's ideas did not matter unless one reconsidered them in the light of one's own personal experience. The principal belief by which George and Charles Ives lived was stated simply by Emerson: "Nothing is at last sacred but the integrity of your own mind."

Because George Ives was the leader of a number of town bands, both in Danbury and in neighboring villages, he was able to do things other band leaders could not. Often on holidays like Memorial Day or the Fourth of July, the bands would all come to Danbury for a musical celebration. But George Ives was not satisfied merely to have the bands march up and down the street playing. On a few occasions he experimented with placing the bands in different locations, which created an antiphonal, or echo effect, when they played. Sometimes he even had the groups play different tunes in different keys, all at the same time. We can imagine how the spectators reacted to such performances! But these experiments had a tremendous effect on Charlie. Much of his later music recalls these events he witnessed as a child. His well-known *Three Places in New England* includes a section depicting in sound a Fourth of July picnic at Putnam's Camp in Redding, Connecticut, with two bands playing two different marches in different keys, creating the kind of clash that George Ives's bands had produced.

At the age of ten, Charlie was already feeling the urge to write his own music, probably because of his father's creative method of teaching. One of his first pieces was a funeral march for the family cat, Chin-Chin, which gained him some measure of fame. Before long he was being asked to write more dirges for deceased pets around the neighborhood. One of these compositions, "Slow March," was based on an aria from Handel's oratorio *Saul*, which he had often admired. This song appeared many years later in the volume *114 Songs*, which contains some of the best examples of Ives's vocal music.

On Memorial Day 1888, the Danbury band played "Holiday Quickstep," a march that Charlie had composed a few months earlier. The composer, however, was too embarrassed to take his usual place in the band with his snare drum, and instead he stayed home to play handball and did not even look up as the band went by his house on Main Street.

Why was Charlie so embarrassed about his musical accomplishments? As a good athlete, and concerned about what his classmates thought of him, he was quite sensitive to comments that writing or playing music was "sissy." He was so aware of this opinion among most boys of his own age that, as a friend humorously reported later, often when people asked what he played, meaning what musical instrument, he would answer curtly, "I play shortstop."

Perhaps some of his embarrassment was overcome after the performance of the march, which was a real success in the town. It brought Charlie a lot of recognition among the townspeople, and he was surely pleased about that. His name appeared in the local newspaper, and he was praised warmly for his accomplishments.

Music was not, however, his only talent. Much like his father, he had developed a number of interests outside of music, and remained a well-rounded person throughout his life. At Danbury Academy and Danbury High School, people looked up to Charles. He was well-liked by his teachers and his friends and was a responsible person who naturally took on positions of leadership, although he was generally quiet and modest. Charles was best known for his achievements in sports. He was captain of the football team at both the Academy and the High School, and also played baseball, as a pitcher and a shortstop, and tennis. He took his sports activities almost as seriously as his music, which may be one of the reasons his music has such vibrant energy in it.

Charles did reasonably well in school, although he

was not a star student. Part of the reason he was not was that his musical activities were so time-consuming.

In addition to everything else, at a very early age Charlie had become an organist of some renown. He began his study of the organ at the age of eleven, and by the time he was thirteen he had a regular job as organist at the West Street Congregational Church in Danbury. He gave organ recitals, in addition to writing organ pieces, songs and instrumental compositions. After one of his recitals at the Baptist Church in 1888, the Danbury newspaper hailed him as "the youngest organist in the state." Two years later, after giving another recital, in which he played pieces by Rossini, Bach and Mendelssohn, among others, Charlie's achievements were again praised in the local paper. The small notice read:

Master Ives deserves and receives great praise for his patient perseverence in his study of the organ, and is to be congratulated on his marked ability as a master of the keys for one so young. We predict for him a brilliant future as an organist.

Probably the writer of the notice in the Danbury paper did not know that young Ives was equally talented as a composer and a pianist, and that as a sixteen-year-old, he already possessed a mature musician's knowledge of his subject.

When he was seventeen, Charles wrote a piece that has since become one of his most famous works. This was the *Variations on "America"*, his first experimental piece. Even today it sounds quite "modern," for the five variations for organ on the national hymn included interludes that were "polytonal," that is, they used two keys at the same time. This method of writing was directly related to George Ives's earlier experiments with "Swanee River" and other melodies. However, the music was not often performed in its full version because not many people were accustomed to such "harsh" sounds. When Charles played the piece in organ recitals he gave in Danbury and nearby Brewster, New York, his father made him cut out the polytonal interludes because they "made the boys laugh out loud and get noisy."

In spite of all the time he spent on music and sports, Charlie still had time to be with people. He was a person of keen intellect who could hold his own among most people his own age and older. His creative outlook showed up in almost everything he did.

Socially Charles had few problems. He never had a lack of good friends, although they didn't all understand how he could spend so much time practicing and writing music. But Charles chose not to let his friends

Charles Ives (left) in 1894, as the pitcher of the Hopkins School baseball team, with a teammate. PHOTOGRAPH COURTESY JOHN HERRICK JACKSON MUSIC LIBRARY, YALE UNIVERSITY.

get too involved with that, and put great energies into being a "regular" guy. Aside from his cousins, Amelia and Sarane, however, he was shy with girls, even though he was admired for his lean good looks.

After Charles graduated from High School, he went to Hopkins Preparatory School in New Haven for a year, a common practice for boys who wanted to attend one of the Ivy League universities of the East.

One story people still like to tell today is that at Hopkins, he pitched for the baseball team that beat the Yale freshmen, an occasion that prompted a great celebration at the school.

There was an understanding among the young men of the Ives family that they would attend Yale University. And so, in 1894, a little bit nervous but wealthy with family and intellectual experiences, Charlie set off for Yale.

3

Yale Years

"For God, for Country, and for Yale." Thus ended a Yale song—one that was probably sung many times by Charles Ives and his school buddies. In 1894, when Charles was a freshman, Yale College in New Haven already had 193 years of glorious history to look back on. It had become a firm part of New England tradition and could boast of numerous well-known politicians, businessmen and other men in the public eye among its alumni.

Love of country and of school was very important at Yale, along with the preservation of old school traditions. Unlike its rival, Harvard, Yale generally frowned upon individualism. Everyone at Yale knew that the spirit of community and conformity was more highly valued than the pursuit of originality and there were few, if any, personal rivalries. So it may seem a bit peculiar that an individualist like Ives could have felt at home at Yale. But Ives's personality had an unusual two-sidedness. It allowed him on one hand to be a strong nonconformist, and on the other to adjust quite well to rules and accepted modes of behavior.

For many years Yale had played an important role in the Ives family. There were thirteen Iveses before Charles who attended the school; and like his relatives before him, Charles was quickly subjected to the strict academic atmosphere of the college. He could no longer enjoy the freedom his earlier studies had allowed. The amount of time to be spared from regular academic courses was limited. As a freshman he was studying Greek, Latin, mathematics and German and English literature.

This is not to say that there was no time for music. Because he was not necessarily interested in being a top student in his other subjects, he did have time to pursue his musical interests. His principal musical courses were organ and composition. For organ his teacher was Dudley Buck, one of the most prominent organist-composers of nineteenth century America. Charles also obtained more practical experience as an organist by finding a job at the Center Church in New Haven, which he kept for four years.

Horatio Parker taught the composition class that Charles attended, and here he had the benefit of learning from one of the most respected American musicians of the time. Parker was known throughout the country for a number of fine religious works. But he was a stern traditionalist when it came to composition. He frowned upon attempts at originality in music when they overstepped the textbook rules. Even though Charles wrote many works at Yale that did not follow the rulebook, he attended Parker's class with a good tolerance and respect for his teacher's opinions. This respect for tradition and discipline no doubt came from his upbringing, and the example set by his family.

Seventy-six South Middle Street was the address of Connecticut Hall, where Charles lived for his four Yale years with his roommate Mandeville Mullally. Ives had many other close friends at Yale, most of whom continued to be his friends for years after.

One of Ives's good friends at Yale was his future brother-in-law, Dave Twichell, who hoped to study medicine. With him and other friends, Charles enjoyed an active social life. He played football and baseball. He also joined three private societies—which were a mark of social success—among them the honored Wolf's Head.

Ives's Yale friends referred to him fondly by a number of nicknames, and his later friend Henry Cowell suggested that the nicknames emphasized different aspects of his personality—Dasher ("the spontaneous and explosive Ives"), Lemuel ("the ascetic New Englander"), Quigg ("the crotchety Quixote"), and Sam ("the punster and joker addicted to paradoxes"). These characterizations are quite apt, for Ives was a person whose personality was as creative as his music.

Charles's college years were not without their sadnesses. Three weeks after he entered Yale, his father died. He was struck with the natural sense of loss at the death of a parent, but this was intensified by a second loss, for his father had for many years been his greatest supporter and source of encouragement. Who was there now to boost him in his work?

He was lucky to find a close friend in John Cornelius Griggs, the choirmaster and baritone at Center Church, where Ives was the organist. Griggs was a family man like Charles's father and saw that Charles still needed an older man to come to for advice and encouragement. The support he gave Charles during the four years at Yale was extraordinary, both in music and in personal matters. Many years later the composer wrote:

> After Father's death Dr. Griggs . . . was the only musician friend of mine that showed any interest, toleration, or tried to understand the way I felt about some things in music . . .

Griggs, unlike Horatio Parker, encouraged Charles in his more unusual experiments with composition, although there were probably many times when he did not fully understand them. There was no one really who could take the place of George Ives, no one who could understand so well Charles's musical and artistic ideas.

Griggs also gave Ives the opportunity to have his music heard. In addition to occasionally singing some of the young composer's songs, he encouraged Charles to play his own music on the church organ, even when the congregation did not approve of what they were hearing. Ives's music was different from anything they had encountered before, especially in church. It often contained unusual harmonies and dissonances—sounds they didn't think fit together.

But Griggs said, "Never you mind what the ladies' committee says, my opinion is that God must get awfully tired of hearing the same thing over and over again, and in his all-embracing wisdom he could certainly embrace a dissonance—might even positively enjoy one now and then."

The only other source of practical experience for Ives was the Hyperion Theatre orchestra. Both the leader and some of the members knew Charles well and were willing to try out some of his new pieces—including some overtures and marches, brass band pieces, and short orchestra pieces.

Frequently Ives would play piano, as he and the other men improvised together—often in a then popular style called ragtime, which has a catchy, offbeat rhythm. A few of Ives's later pieces like the "Theater Orchestra Set" and "A Yale–Princeton Football Game" are reminiscent of these college "jam sessions."

The experience he gained working with the Hyperion Orchestra meant a great deal to him. Even though these performances were more like rehearsals than concert performances, Ives maintained for years that they were the genuine premieres of certain pieces, which in some cases were not officially premiered for forty or more years.

His experiences in making music with Griggs and with the Hyperion Orchestra were important in his development as a composer. But it was Horatio Parker who actually molded Charles's musical education during the years at Yale, even when teacher and student did not agree. Parker, like most other American musicians of his time, had been educated in Europe, and like most of these traditional musicians, did not like experimentation in music. According to them, music had to be written with the models of the great German, French and Italian masters constantly in mind.

There was some value in this method of writing music, because it taught certain basic truths of harmony and structure, but it certainly did not allow a composer to use new ideas. The Americans had failed to realize that music, like all the other arts, was constantly changing and evolving. Their insistence on slavishly following old forms stifled the use of fresh ideas in composition, which would have kept American music alive. In one of Ives's memos of later years he devised a motto for these people: "All things have a right to live and grow, even babies and music schools—but not music!"

Even the Europeans thought that the Americans were too strict in following forms of music that originated in other countries. Many of them felt that the Americans should look to their own folk and popular music for inspiration, so that their compositions would really be their own. The French composer Vincent d'Indy was once reported to have said to a friend of Ives:

Why don't your American composers inspire themselves from their own landscapes, their own legends and history, instead of leaning forever on the German walking-stick?

Early in his freshman year, Ives showed Parker some of his compositions done in a free, experimental style. Among these were a fugue for organ in four keys and the choral piece, "Psalm 67," in two keys. Probably Parker had never seen music like this before, and undoubtedly never wanted to again. He simply asked Ives not to bring that kind of piece to class. So after the first few weeks of his freshman year, Ives didn't bother bringing his experimental pieces to class because Parker disliked them so much. Yet always in the back of Charles's mind was the fact that his father had welcomed seeing such compositions and had been willing to help Charles work them out.

Ives showed Parker only the compositions that were more or less traditional, and Parker did give him advice in composing music of this kind that was definitely valuable. One cannot write really good music without having a solid background in the classics and in the traditional forms of music, and this Ives obtained primarily through his study with Horatio Parker.

The amount of music Ives wrote as a Yale student is incredible, especially when one realizes that he was also studying the regular academic subjects. He spent so much time and energy writing music, it is a wonder he had as many friends as he did. Many of them had no idea of the scope of his writing. There were songs, instrumental pieces, orchestral marches and overtures and choral pieces, as well as the First String Quartet and the First Symphony written during his college years.

The First String Quartet was written in 1896 for a revival service at Center Church; hence the names of the four movements: "Chorale," "Prelude," "Offertory" and "Postlude." Compared to some of Ives's other pieces, this one was quite mild, because it did not use any obvious experimental forms or harmonies. Even so Parker disapproved, for he did not like the idea of using hymn tunes in serious music, a practice Charles employed quite often. Parker also thought the harmonies were a bit daring. Our modern ears are accustomed to the kinds of sounds Ives used in the quartet, but they were somewhat unusual for their time.

The first movement of the quartet is a very stirring and beautiful piece in the form of a fugue, based on the hymn "From Greenland's Icy Mountains." Ives was quite fond of incorporating melodies he had known since childhood into his music. In a similar fashion, he often used music he had written earlier as material for new pieces. The fugue from the First String Quartet, for example, was rewritten twenty years later and appears in the third movement of his huge Fourth Symphony. The largo of the Second Symphony was also based on a section of the First String Quartet.

The First Symphony, also written at Yale, was a truly remarkable achievement for a young composer. In recent years it has received many performances and has been recorded a number of times by some of the country's best orchestras. Yet when Charles showed the first movement to Parker, it was strongly criticized. In Parker's opinion, Charles had been too free in his use of different keys. Charles's way of explaining this was to say, "the boys got going."

"Ives, why must you hog all the keys?" Parker asked. So Charles wrote a second version in a more conservative style that pleased Parker, but not himself. He maintained that the first version was the better one.

Despite Parker's criticisms, Ives held the man in respect throughout his life. He was later to write:

I had and have great respect and admiration for Parker and most of his music (It was seldom trivial—his choral works have a dignity and depth that many of [his] contemporaries did not have.), but he was governed too much by the German rule, and in some ways was somewhat hard boiled.

At Yale Charles didn't restrict himself to writing "serious" music. He had a kind of musical talent that could adapt itself to many different styles so he could and did compose and arrange patriotic music for the school. "The Bells of Yale" and "A Song of Mory's" were among these pieces. They are delightful songs, very much in the style of popular nineteenth century music. Ives's friends thought this music was first-rate and were quite impressed with Charles's talents. Few of them knew that he was also a serious composer.

The social clubs and fraternities at Yale often put on theatrical shows, frequently in a humorous vein. Charles was also involved in these, and wrote music for the shows. One such presentation by the fraternity Delta Kappa Epsilon, was entitled "Hells Bells" and featured original music by "Mr. C. E. Ives."

The year 1897 saw the composition of what Charles thought was his "first serious piece quite away from the German rule book." This was the organ *Prelude and Postlude for a Thanksgiving Service*, which he played at Center Church in November. Like some of his earlier pieces, it had sections that used different keys at the same time. This was done partly out of reverence for his forefathers—Charles felt such harmonies represented the Puritan ideal of sternness and strength. It was the first experimental piece he was really proud of, and a few years later he arranged a portion of it for orchestra to incorporate into his *New England Holidays* symphony.

Parker attended the performance, but he did not think much of the composition. Ives told an anecdote about the performance.

Parker made some fairly funny cracks about it, but Dr. Griggs said it had something of

"HELLS BELLS,"

—OR—

The Fight that Yaled.

For the last time the '98 extravaganza company presents the rib-fracturing phantasy of which the headlines appear above. This mammoth production over which no time and expense have been wasted, brings to a culminating climax the apex of our efforts.

Mr. C. E. Ives has furnished much original music for this play; his latest masterpiece will be sung at the close of the 3rd Act. The words were written by F. G. Hinsdale. You are all requested to join in the chorus, but kindly wait until it sounds familiar.

HAIL TO PHI.

All of our labors over now,
    Times of parting come to all ;
Come they must,
    Strengthen here the vow,
Phi the brotherhood,
    Altar of our faith and trust ;
Some of our brothers moving on,
    Forth to face the restless world
Life's stern fight,
    All their sorrows, cares and troubles gone ;
Gone, alas ! their days in Phi so bright.

Hail to Phi, its blaze of glory,
    Never will grow cold,
Dear to all thy children's hearts,
    Ever faithful as of old.
All our days we'll love thee, never fail,
    When we feel in after life
Chill fortune round us fold,
    Then we'll hasten back to Phi and Yale.
Hail to Phi ! Hail to Phi !
    Strong the bond. Strong the bond,
Likewise Yale the Alma Mater.

PLAY COMMITTEE.

HINSDALE.   BORDEN.   IVES.
    KENNEDY.   SIMMONS.   WADSWORTH.

This play was written by Hinsdale, Kennedy, Wadsworth.

VALE.

The program of a Yale fraternity show, for which Ives supplied the music. PHOTOGRAPH COURTESY JOHN HERRICK JACKSON MUSIC LIBRARY, YALE UNIVERSITY.

34

the Puritan character, a stern but outdoors strength, and something of the pioneering feeling. He liked it as such, and told Parker so. Parker just smiled and took him over to Heublein's for a beer.

In retrospect Parker's lack of respect for Ives's musical ideas seems careless. But the truth is that it would have been unusual for almost anyone to understand the kinds of things Ives was doing in the 1890s, for it was all astonishingly original and advanced for its time. Ives did not know it at that time, but he would have to wait more than twenty years before more than a handful of people would begin to understand his music.

4

Early Years
in New York

"Poverty Flat" was the nickname of the large apartment
in New York where Ives lived with a number of friends
after his graduation from Yale. It was 1898 when Charles
joined some young men already in the building on West
58th Street. Poverty Flat had become the residence of a
number of Yale graduates who were studying in New
York and wanted to live economically in a kind of com-
munal situation.

At Poverty Flat most of the men were studying
medicine, but the group was rounded out by a few law
students and a few men who were just starting business
careers. This was a good cross section of Yale graduates,
because these were the three fields most Yale men went
into. Even Ives, who was one of the handful of music
students at Yale, had decided to give the business world
a try.

Ives's decision not to try to earn a living as a composer, but to enter business instead, was not a hasty one. It had come after many hours of deep thought. As a child he had experienced a rich family life, and from this had come a desire to have a family of his own. To do this he felt he had to find a job that would give him a good, stable income.

Unfortunately this did not seem possible for a professional composer. Few composers then, or since, have received steady and sufficient income from their work. It would have been especially difficult for a composer like Ives, whose music was so unusual, to support a family from his composition alone, especially since he was not interested in taming his music to please the public's tastes. He was well aware of the fact that his was not the kind of music that could ever become "popular." As a result, he gave up the idea of being a professional musician and decided to go into another field where his efforts would be more justly rewarded.

This idea came partly from his father, and in explaining his position he wrote:

Father felt that a man could keep his music-interest stronger, cleaner, bigger and freer, if he didn't try to make a living out of it. Assuming a man lived by himself and with no dependents, no one to feed but himself and willing to live as simply as Thoreau—(he) might write music that no one would play, publish, listen to, or buy. But—if he has a nice wife and some nice children, how can he let the children starve on his dissonances?

In addition, Charles remembered clearly his family's situation when he was growing up, and these memories made him even more firm in his decision about going into business. Life had not been easy for the family when George Ives had tried to earn a living solely as a musician. His position and income were never very stable, and the family often had to struggle to make ends meet. Later George Ives had taken a position with the Danbury Bank in order to give his family greater financial security. Of course, he was not as happy working in a bank as he had been as a full-time musician, but his worries were fewer. When Charles reflected on this later, he knew his father had been wise.

With all this in mind, Ives fashioned a plan for his new life in New York. He would find a job with one of the big insurance companies. At that time they were just beginning to expand, and he felt he could probably get himself into a position that would give him good opportunities for advancement. A short time after moving to Poverty Flat, he found his first job, as a clerk in the actuarial department of the Mutual Life Insurance Company. This was in the summer of 1898. The actuarial department was in charge of keeping statistics on the company and on the people who held their policies. For his work there Ives received a salary of five dollars per week.

Nowadays we look on the insurance business a bit more cynically than people did in the early part of the century. Although one cannot deny that big business then had many of the same problems as it does today, people's attitudes toward it were different. There was room in it for a bit of nineteenth century idealism, and this is what Ives brought to his job and eventually to the whole life insurance business.

Charles was fascinated with his job because it allowed him to explore the area that most interested him outside of his music—the plight of the common man. Every day he was confronted with the raw materials of people's lives: what kind of work they did; how much money they earned; how they supported their families. He soon saw clearly what could happen if a person were to die and leave a family with no support. This convinced him that life insurance was something of value to all people, regardless of their economic class, and he devoted his career to discovering and promoting ways of reaching people with the idea that life insurance could be beneficial to them.

His business talents and interest in his work did not

go unnoticed. Within a year Ives was transferred to the Raymond Agency of the Mutual Life Insurance Company, at 32 Liberty Street. His new job was as applications clerk, and his salary was increased to about one hundred dollars a month.

He was brought into the agency to take over the job of a man named Julian Myrick. The two men soon became friends. But Myrick said that Ives's handwriting was so bad that they were forced to trade places. Myrick became applications clerk again, and Charles moved over to handling the agents—the men who actually sold the insurance. Ives was better suited to this job, which was a good deal more creative than working with numbers and statistics.

Charles's ambition and energy was extraordinary. In addition to working at Mutual Life with exceptional enthusiasm, he devoted almost all of his free time to his music. After work he rushed home to the piano, and there he would work at composition, often until two in the morning. The only break he had was for supper with his roommates, and an occasional concert at Carnegie Hall.

Unlike most other musicians, Ives was not an enthusiastic concert goer. In part, he felt he could not afford to take time away from his composing. He also did not want to have other people's music interfering with his own. He explained it best himself:

. . . On account of having only a limited time in which to work, I got into the habit of carrying things in my mind which were not put down, or only partly put down, on paper. As this was the case most of the time, I found that listening to music (especially if in the programs there were things with which I was not familiar) tended to throw me out of my stride. . . .

At any rate, I found that I could work more naturally and with more concentration if I didn't hear much music, especially unfamiliar music. To make a long story short, I went to very few concerts. I suppose everyone is built differently and works differently. It just so happened that I felt I could work better and like to work more, if I kept to my own music and let other people keep to theirs.

Some years ago there were people who criticized Ives because he did not keep up with the rest of the musical world. They felt his music would have been more accessible and logical if he had paid attention to other musicians and their work. But most people have now come to realize how important Ives's decision to isolate himself was. It was one of the primary reasons he became the great musical pioneer he did. There are and have always been many fine composers who imitate the musical styles of the day, but the few who create their own style are the ones we remember. Ives became one of these.

Even for Ives, relief from the long hours of composition was needed, and he liked to share his musical ability. Since for many years he had enjoyed his work as a church organist, he saw no reason why he should not continue this in New York. It would also make his financial situation, which was a little difficult when he first moved to New York, a bit easier. He found a job at the Central Presbyterian Church, which then was not too far from Poverty Flat, as the organist and choir director. This meant he was responsible for almost all the musical activities of the church. In general it worked out quite well, but he had trouble finding enough male voices for the choir. Most of the time he could persuade his housemates to help him out by coming to church and singing, but they were usually not too happy about it.

With as much experience with church music as he had had, it seems logical that it should have been a real source of musical inspiration to him. Ives particularly loved the many hymns he had known since childhood and played in church over the years. But being familiar with them did not mean he was content to continually play them exactly as they were written. He would ornament his playing with extra notes that were not in the traditional harmony. To him this was an imitation of how one might hear a hymn played or sung outdoors, with nature's sounds supplying the extra notes. It also made the music seem much stronger, because the meaning of the words was intensified by the unusual harmonies.

He hoped the Central Presbyterian congregation would not take too much notice of these changes. But they were more attentive than he imagined, and protests arose occasionally. People wanted to hear the old hymns just as they had always been heard. Reluctantly, Ives listened to his superiors at the church and tried to play the music just as it was written, but it was difficult for him.

Ives was not the first composer to have such problems—the conflict between a church congregation's ideas of music and a composer's ideas has long troubled musicians. The two have never been able to agree. Almost two hundred years before Ives's time, Johann Sebastian Bach was the victim of similar disputes. Much of the music he had written for the church in Leipzig, Germany, was considered too progressive by the church officials. They could not know, of course, that the music they were hearing was going to profoundly influence the music of the future. Similarly, although on a smaller scale, Ives's congregation did not know that they were witnessing the birth of some of the most original musical ideas of the twentieth century.

Despite these problems, Ives maintained his deep love for Protestant church music, and incorporated much of it into his music. Hymns were especially important to his Third Symphony, The Camp Meeting, which he worked on during his early years in New York. Many of its themes were based on music Ives played at Central Presbyterian Church around the year 1901.

The first movement of the symphony, entitled "Old Folks Gathern'," borrows the tune of the hymn "What a Friend We Have in Jesus." In the second movement, "Children's Day," Ives weaves the music around the melody "There is a Fountain Filled with Blood." Finally, in the last movement, "Communion," he uses the tune for "Just As I Am Without One Plea." The skillful and original way the hymns are woven into the symphonic texture creates a beautiful impression of a nineteenth century camp meeting, where people would gather to sing hymns and express their devotion. The symphony ends with the ethereal sounds of church bells ringing in the distance.

Although the symphony was finished around 1904, it did not receive its premiere until Lou Harrison conducted it in 1947 with the New York Little Symphony Orchestra. As a result of this performance, Ives received the Pulitzer Prize, the highest honor an American composer can achieve. When Ives received the prize, he could not help but think of the irony of it, for the symphony's merits had been discovered long before, in 1911, by the great Austrian composer and conductor Gustav Mahler.

Mahler came across the score one day when it was being worked on at Tams, a firm to which Ives sent much of his music to be copied. Mahler was impressed with what he saw, and indicated that he would like to conduct the work in Europe. Unfortunately Mahler died the same year, and the performance was never given. Many have imagined how different Ives's career might have been if Mahler had conducted the Third Symphony in 1911. There can be little doubt that people would at least have been interested in hearing some of his other works.

Because of his involvement with the church, Ives also wrote anthems for church choirs. Few of these works were performed at the time he was writing them. They include settings for a number of Psalms from the Bible; among the better known of these today are Psalms 67, 90, 100 and 150. Other religious choral works included the prelude "Let There Be Light" and the magnificent "Three Harvest Home Chorales," for double chorus, organ and brass.

It was natural that some of his religious compositions began to get attention, although Ives did not actively seek it. And in a few cases there were formal performances. One of these was in April of 1902, the premiere of his recently composed church cantata, the *Celestial Country* .

The seven movements of the piece were scored for mixed chorus, solo quartet, strings, brass and organ. A number of instrumental and vocal combinations were used, all based on popular musical forms for religious works—among them organ preludes, solo arias and choral hymns. Ives used Henry Alford's "Processional Hymn" as a text.

Although the cantata was rather traditional when compared to some of Ives's other pieces, it did contain some strikingly original ideas. Its greatest merit lay in its highly effective use of all the vocal and instrumental resources it called for. Because of this, the performers were pleased with the music, for it displayed their talents well.

As is customary for important premieres, a reporter from the *New York Times* was sent to review the concert. In his opinion:

". . . the composition . . has the elementary merits of being scholarly and well made. But it is also spirited and melodious, and with a full chorus should be as effective in the whole as it was on this occasion in some of the details."

Another summary of the concert appeared in the *Musical Courier*, the oldest of American musical periodicals. In addition to discussing some of the unusual smaller aspects of the piece, the article said:

> The works shows undoubted earnestness in study, and talent for composition. . . . Beginning with a prelude, trio and chorus, with soft, long-drawn chords of mysterious meaning . . . the music swells to a fine climax . . . throughout the work there is homogeneity, coming from the interweaving of appropriate themes."

Why such an enthusiastic reception for Ives? Undoubtedly part of the reason both reviewers were pleased with the work was that it showed very few "modern" tendencies. Ives's old teacher Horatio Parker probably would have liked it, too, for it did not contain strange musical experiments. In fact, the cantata is very similar to Parker's own *Hora Novissima* an oratorio that was once popular, but seldom performed today.

It is ironic that music critics could see Ives's talent when he imitated others, but would no doubt have been shocked by his more original work.

47

5

New Musical Discoveries, The Life Insurance Business and Harmony

As Ives became more and more involved in composing, certain characteristics began to crystalize in his music. The primary characteristic that contributed to its extreme originality was its dissonance.

Dissonance, at its simplest, can be defined as sounds that clash with each other: but a better description would be sounds that create tension in music, for our ideas about what sounds *are* dissonant are always changing. In the late nineteenth century and early twentieth centuries, European as well as other American composers were experimenting with dissonance. The Austrian Arnold Schoenberg and the Russian Igor Stravinsky were, perhaps, the two most notable of these. Their approach was quite different from Ives. Most of the music of the Europeans was a natural outgrowth of nineteenth century trends and styles. For example, Schoenberg's music can be traced almost directly from the music of Wagner, Mahler and Richard Strauss. Stravinsky was influenced by both the French school (Debussy) and the Russian school (Rimsky-Korsakov, Mussoursky).

Ives's music, however did not grow smoothly out of an accepted style. It was a mixture of many different musical impressions, and in many instances used popular music rather than art music as its basis. Because of this, it is possible to say that his experiments with new musical ideas were, in a way, more original than those of his European contemporaries.

In the 1891 *Variations on "America"* and the 1897 *Prelude and Postlude for a Thanksgiving Service*, Ives made his first important experiments with dissonance. He achieved his effects by using two or more keys at the same time, a phenomenon we call polytonality. Aside from the fact that he was fascinated with the new sounds he was making, Ives used polytonality in his pieces because he felt it represented "the sternness and strength and austerity of the Puritan character." It had the same qualities of character building as the "ear-stretching" techniques his father had taught him in his earlier years. Ives also thought that the usual major, minor and diminished chords were too easy to listen to. In his words, they gave "too much a feeling of bodily ease, which the Puritan did not give in to."

The Puritan austerity of the music was the perfect

complement in many cases to the words of some of Ives's vocal pieces. A good example is the "Psalm 67," in which two choirs simultaneously sing in two different keys the following words:

God be merciful unto us,
And bless us;
And cause his face to shine upon us;
That thy way may be known upon earth,
Thy saving health among all nations.

Let the people praise thee, O God;
Let all the people praise thee.
O Let the nations be glad and sing for joy;
For thou shalt judge the people righteously,
And govern the nations upon the earth.

Let the people praise thee, O God;
Let all the people praise thee.

Then shall the earth yield her increase;
And God, Even our own God,
Shall bless us.

God shall bless us;
And all the ends of the earth shall fear him.

Later, Ives used polytonality to create complex, dissonant pieces of music in which different groups play against one another in a sort of "collision of musical events," as one Ives enthusiast has put it. Stravinsky began using polytonality at about the same time. In his ballets *Petrushka* (1911) and the *Rite of Spring* (1913) he used two keys simultaneously and as musical devices they have a powerful effect: but they do not influence the whole character of the composition, they are not the essence of the work, as they are in Ives. Compared to Ives's "Thanksgiving" and "Washington's Birthday" from the Holidays Symphony, Stravinsky's ballets sound almost orderly. Ives's music is often an intentionally disorderly conglomerate of musical ideas, all stated simultaneously. In later years people often talked about this as one of Ives's most important contributions to music. To this day, the word "Ivesian" conjures up a picture of frantic and varied musical impressions, seemingly unrelated and unorganized, producing in music some of the same effects double or triple exposures produce visually on a roll of photographic film.

All this musical experimentation before too long brought to an end Ives's career as a church musician. After just a few years in New York, he was beginning to feel that the routine music he was obliged to play each Sunday for services and with the choir at rehearsals was hindering his musical development. He hungered to re-create music, not just play the notes. But because the congregation of the church was not open to new concepts of music, he couldn't try out the ideas that were constantly in his head and wanting to be worked out.

Of course, there was only one solution to his predicament—give up the job. This he did in 1902. It was probably done with a bit of sadness, for he had given almost fifteen years to the church, and had certainly benefited from the experience. But at the same time, it was a relief not to have to worry about the "nice" congregation that didn't want to put up with any "modern music." He found that his composing went better when he didn't have to adjust his thinking to church music several times a week. He wrote, "I seemed to have worked (in composition) with more natural freedom when I knew that the music was not going to be played before the public, or rather before people who couldn't get out from under, as is the case of a church congregation. . . ."

In music and in business, Ives's single-mindedness and complete devotion to his work were the key to his achievements. But his success in business was recognized long before his success in music. By the time he was thirty, people in business were becoming familiar with his name.

By late in the year 1906, Ives felt sufficiently knowledgeable and experienced to want to go into business for himself. He had worked for the Raymond Agency of the Mutual Life Insurance Company for eight years, and felt he knew what he had to know. In January of 1907, he and his friend Julian Myrick set up the offices of Ives and Company at 51 Liberty Street in downtown Manhattan. It was not long before the agency, which in 1909 was reorganized as Ives & Myrick, was the most prosperous in the city, primarily because the talents of the two men complimented each other well. At the age of twenty-seven, Myrick had gained sufficient respect among his colleagues to be elected secretary of the Life Underwriter's Association of the City of New York, and eight years later he was named its president. Myrick was known in the business world for many years as "Mr. Life Insurance."

Ives was the creative genius behind the agency. He devoted hours and hours to writing pamphlets of advice for young insurance agents, all with the same goal in mind—to convince as many people as possible that life insurance could be valuable to them and their families. In his pamphlet, "The Amount to Carry," Ives summarized his idealistic attitude to the life insurance business:

It can be said . . . that the development of life insurance, particularly in the manner of presenting its services to the public and in increas-

Where $15,000,000 Was Paid For Last Year

The picture shown above is of the corner of the building at Nassau and Liberty Streets, New York City, where more life insurance was written last year than in any other general agency office in New York. Just above the entrance are the offices of IVES & MYRICK, managers of the MUTUAL LIFE, who paid for more than $15,000,000.

Advertisement for the Ives and Myrick Company. PHOTOGRAPH COURTESY JOHN HERRICK JACKSON MUSIC LIBRARY, YALE UNIVERSITY.

ing the benefits, has become more and more
scientific in its worth. That is, the fundamental
in each essential premise has become clearer to
more minds. Life insurance is doing its part in
the progress of the greater life values.

"The Amount To Carry" was a basic text for the life
insurance agents who worked for Ives & Myrick. In a
training school the firm set up for agents, the men were
taught the techniques Ives explained in his writings. This
training school was one of the most successful innova-
tions of the firm, and within a few years it had become
a standard part of most of the large insurance companies
in the country.

The agency's great success was also due to the close
feeling among its employees. This started at the top with
the close friendship of Charles Ives and Julian Myrick.
Not only were the two men good friends at work, but
they also saw each other outside of work. Both were enthusiastic about sports, and they occasionally got together with a few of the other men from Poverty Flat
for a ballgame in Central Park. Both had enormous respect for each other. Myrick had a deep admiration for
Ives's dedication to his music, and could not speak highly
enough of his business talents: "He (Ives) had a great
conception of the life insurance business and what it

could and should do; and had a powerful way of expressing it."

Although Ives was an extraordinarily busy and ambitious person, not every minute of his time was spent working. He loved to get away from the city and go to someplace where the air was cleaner and the scenery more beautiful. Often he went to Pine Mountain, near Danbury, where his family owned some land. He and his brother Moss, and occasionally some of his roommates from Poverty Flat, went camping there; and in about 1903 they built a small cabin.

Much of the time when he was at Pine Mountain, Ives simply enjoyed the outdoors, often reflecting on the ideas of his great hero, Henry David Thoreau. One of the most famous passages of Thoreau's *Walden*, which Ives read and reread many times, went like this:

> I went to the woods because I wished to live
> deliberately, to front only the essential facts of
> life, and see if I could not learn what it had to
> teach, and not, when I came to die, discover
> that I had not lived. . . . I wanted to live deep
> and suck out all the marrow of life, to live so
> sturdily and Spartanlike as to put to rout all
> that was not life, to cut a broad swath and
> shave close, to drive life into a corner, and re-

Ives walking in Battery Park, near the office of Ives and Myrick,
around 1917. PHOTOGRAPH COURTESY JOHN HERRICK JACKSON
MUSIC LIBRARY, YALE UNIVERSITY.

duce it to its lowest terms. . . . Simplicity, simplicity, simplicity! I say, let your affairs be as
two or three, and not a hundred or a thousand;
instead of a million count half a dozen, and
keep your accounts on your thumb-nail. . . .
Simplify, simplify.

Although Ives's own life was hardly simple, he believed strongly in Thoreau's criticism of modern society,
and he strived to live up to Thoreau's ideas as best he
could.

Ives also found he could better think out his ideas
about music in the peace and quiet of the country. A
number of his pieces were written or worked on at Pine
Mountain, primarily sections of the *Fourth of July*, the
General Slocum, *Halloween* and the *Alcott Overture*,
which eventually became part of the *Concord Sonata*.
There was also a piece entitled "Autumn Landscape
from Pine Mountain," that has since been lost.

Ives also liked to go to the Adirondack Mountains
in upstate New York with his old friend and Yale class-
mate, Dave Twichell. The Twichell family had for years
gone to a place called Pell Jones, where spectacular
mountains surrounded the lovely, clear Elk Lake. It was
a place in some ways reminiscent of mountain resorts in
Switzerland and Austria.

There, as on Pine Mountain, Ives found that the beautiful setting "inspired" musical composition. Some of the pieces he conceived and worked on at Elk Lake were "Thoreau" from the *Concord Sonata*, the Third Symphony and the Fourth Symphony. They are among his most successful works.

Life during these years was not without its romantic interests, either; for Ives found himself falling in love with Dave Twichell's sister. Charles had always been a bit shy with girls, so this romance, which eventually led to marriage, was probably the only one he had. Appropriately, Dave's sister was named Harmony—people said she was the most beautiful girl in her hometown, Hartford.

Charles and Harmony had first met in the Adirondacks in August of 1896, when Charles was enjoying a two-week vacation as Dave's guest. In the years between 1896 and 1905, when she and Charles met again, Harmony had become a rather accomplished young woman. Like Charles, the household in which she had grown up was in part responsible for the person she had become.

The Twichell home in Hartford had been a frequent meeting place for many important writers of nineteenth century America—among them John Greenleaf Whittier, Charles Dudley Warner, William Dean Howells and

Mark Twain. Harmony's father, Joseph Hopkins Twichell, also a Yale man, was the minister of the Asylum
Hill Church. These writers were among his good friends,
but he was particularly close with Twain, his next door
neighbor. Twain immortalized his friendship with Twichell in his book *A Tramp Abroad*, a delightful account of
a walking tour the two made through southern Germany
and Switzerland in 1878.

Harmony was both artistically sensitive and concerned about the welfare of others. After she was graduated from a girl's school in Farmington, Connecticut,
she studied painting, but then decided that she really
wanted to be a nurse. She attended a nurses training program in Hartford, and then went to Chicago to take her
first professional job. For the next four years she worked
on and off in various places, and when she met Charles
again in 1905, she was employed as a private nurse to
an old friend of her father.

Charles and Harmony began to see each other frequently at Elk Lake, and later in New York City, after
she moved to the city to take a job with the Henry Street
Settlement, an organization devoted to the welfare of less
fortunate persons. Theirs was soon a strong, deep rela-
tionship, often marked by exchanges of poems and music. They worked on a number of pieces together—"Ilmenau" a poem by Goethe, which Harmony translated:
"Spring Song," the "World's Highway" and the "South

Harmony Twichell before her marriage to Charles Ives. PHOTO-
GRAPH COURTESY JOHN HERRICK JACKSON MUSIC LIBRARY, YALE
UNIVERSITY.

Wind," another translation, from Heinrich Heine's poem.

In the fall of 1907 the two announced their plans to marry. Charles loved to tell later of the time during their engagement when Harmony took him to meet Mark Twain, or "Uncle Mark," as she fondly called him. Twain had acted as if Charles were being submitted for his approval, and remarked, "Well, the fore seems to be all right; turn him around and let's see about the aft!"

Their marriage took place in June 1908, in Hartford. Harmony's father performed the ceremony. Afterwards, the wedding party, made up primarily of the two families, attended a reception in the rectory. It must have been obvious to all the guests how well suited these two were to each other. They seemed to balance each other— Charles's excitements and his sometimes eccentric ideas were balanced by Harmony's calm sensibility; and she was probably encouraged by Charles's intense, creative energies to occasionally break through the mildness that had come from her firm and proper upbringing.

Over the years, their life together and with their daughter Edith grew into one of constant devotion, utmost honesty and deep love. Her belief in his music was of enormous importance to him. This can be seen in a few sentences he later wrote:

One thing I am certain of is that, if I have done anything good in music, it was, first because

Harmony and Edith Ives about 1916.

PHOTOGRAPH COURTESY JOHN HERRICK JACKSON MUSIC LIBRARY, YALE UNIVERSITY.

of my father, and second, because of my wife. What she has done for me I won't put down, because she won't let me. But I am going to put this down at least: —After any of these musical friends of mine had left, she never once said or suggested or looked or thought that there must be something wrong with me—a thing implied, if not expressed, by most everybody else, including members of the family. She never said, "Now why don't you be good, and write something nice the way they like it?"—Never! She urged me on my way—to be myself! She gave me not only help but a confidence that no one else since father had given me.

6

Ives In His Prime

Few composers can work steadily and confidently without some kind of communication from the public, whether the reaction is negative or positive. Gustav Mahler reached the high point of his composing career when he was in his forties and was recognized as one of the great musical geniuses of his time, even though reaction to him ranged from bitter hatred to worshiping love. Arnold Schoenberg's career followed this same pattern. Even composers like Schubert, who remains a classic example of the composer unrecognized in his lifetime, were known and respected in the most important musical circles of their time.

But Ives's development as a composer was quite unusual and clearly out of step with this normal process. The high point of his creative life did not in any way coincide with his recognition as a composer. He was about forty years old when he wrote his most significant works, but his music then was unknown to all but his wife and a few friends. His public reputation was based entirely on his being one of the most important men in the life insurance business in the country.

At the same time that the music of Stravinsky, Schoenberg and other musical "revolutionaries" was creating great controversy in Europe, Ives was quietly working in his free time on pieces that were every bit as revolutionary. The difference was that in spite of the public's general disapproval, Stravinsky's and Schoenberg's music was being performed, in many cases by the best performers and ensembles in Europe.

During the years from 1906 to 1916, when such extraordinarily original works as Stravinsky's *Rite of Spring*, Schoenberg's *Pierre Lunaire* and Alban Berg's *Five Orchestral Songs* were being premiered in Europe, Ives was hidden away in New York City working on the pieces that would later, along with these, be thought of as landmarks of twentieth century music.

Almost completely isolated from the musical ideas of his contemporaries, he produced such magnificent works as the *Concord Sonata*, the small "cantata" "General William Booth's Entrance into Heaven," the orchestral suite *Three Places in New England*, the *New England Holidays* Symphony, and the astounding and masterful Fourth Symphony. As in all music that we think of as masterpieces, these works achieve a profound synthesis of learned technique, originality, and genuine emotion.

But what specifically were the qualities of Ives's music that make it so significant? We have already seen that he was a pioneer in the use of dissonance, but this alone was not enough to make his music great. Rather, the basis for its greatness seems to lie in the particular and wonderful way he has of illustrating the vastness of man's experience. The music expresses something bigger than itself.

Henry Cowell, a composer who was a very close friend of Ives explained this when he wrote:

> . . . to the Transcendentalist, music is not separate from the rest of the universe but permeates and is in turn permeated by all else that exists. For Ives, music is no more than an expression of the universe than the universe is an expression of music.

Cowell was suggesting that Ives's ideas about music were an extension of the beliefs of the Transcendentalists, a celebrated group of New England writers of the nineteenth century which included Ralph Waldo Emerson and Henry David Thoreau.

Emerson, Thoreau and others in their group

strongly believed in individual idealism, the wisdom of nature and the supreme importance of original ideas. The last of these beliefs was the one that had the most far-reaching effect—it was in part responsible for the growth of American art and culture in the late nineteenth and early twentieth centuries. The very fact that these writers existed seemed to prove that native American culture was as strong and as important as any other. This gave a new self-confidence to all the American artists who followed them. To Ives, born two generations after them, they were a source of confidence in his own work.

In the *Concord Sonata*, now the most famous of his works, Ives expressed the close bond he felt with the New England Transcendentalists. His tribute to them, written during the years 1909-1915, took the form of a piano sonata in four movements, each named for one or more important people in the group: "Emerson," "Hawthorne," "The Alcotts," and "Thoreau." All of these people lived in the town of Concord, Massachusetts.

Concord is one of the most beautiful towns in New England. On its streets marched the Revolutionary War Minutemen, who in April 1775 fought what became the first battle of the war for independence from England. A few miles from the village square, where Emerson's house was the meeting place of some of the most creative minds of the nineteenth century, was the lovely and serene Walden Pond. There the proud twenty-eight-year-old Thoreau built his cabin, planted his bean field and spent two years contemplating and writing about his experiences alone in the woods.

Although Ives's *Concord Sonata* does not tell us anything specific about the transcendentalists, it does illustrate their essential spirit. It seems to say that looking beyond the facts of our everyday lives is more valuable than a constant concern with the trivial.

But how does one portray such a subtle idea in a piece of music? Ives did it by using a musical idea that he found in Beethoven's music, the opening bars of the Fifth Symphony. They contain what Ives called the "universal" or transcendental motive—a four-note motive that had a definite, almost earth-shattering simplicity and firmness.

Ives found that its grand manner seemed to speak to all mankind, and took people beyond their everyday exis-

tence. To Ives, Beethoven was one of the few composers who expressed spiritual strength in his music.

In the *Concord Sonata* the four note motive weaves
its way in and out of the piece constantly, although Ives
never uses it in quite the same way that Beethoven did.
It makes its appearance on the first page, although it is
practically hidden among the rush of other musical ideas
Ives has thrown out at the same time. Its first grand ap-
pearances come a few moments later as the music swells
to a fortissimo:

I. "Emerson"

Throughout the four movements the motive appears in many guises, which are all transformations—permutations—of the original idea. This gives the music variety, but it also ties it together, so that we are left with the impression of a totally unified whole.

The "universal" spirit Ives was after is also achieved by his presentation of a multitude of musical ideas at the beginning, all in the first few measures, which he then sorts and sifts throughout the piece in a completely original way. Because of this sorting and sifting method, the listener is more impressed with the total picture of the composition than with its small details. Through emphasis on the whole rather than the parts, the music does become "transcendental"—a true "expression of the universe."

One's ears must be quick to grasp the fascinating and original spirit of this sonata. But after a few hearings one begins to feel a part of it. It is the most personal kind of music, and this is the reason it has had, over recent years, a tremendous appeal to both performers and listeners. Those who know it, all have their few favorite measures that seem to speak to them directly.

The sonata takes us through, as Ives described it, Emerson's "wider search for the unknowable," Hawthorne's "fantastical adventures," and the "commonplace beauty of the Alcott's 'Orchard House'." The final "picture" of the sonata is of Thoreau playing his flute over Walden Pond, listening to the strange echoes and reverberations it makes, amid the constant accompaniment of nature's sounds. Ives himself described the music by describing Thoreau's thoughts during a day at Walden:

> And if there shall be a program for our music let it follow his thought on an autumn day of Indian summer at Walden . . . he seems to move with the slow, almost monotonous swaying beat of this autumnal day. He is more contented with a "homely burden" and is more assured of "the broad margin to his life;" he sits in his sunny doorway . . . rapt in revery . . . amidst goldenrod, sandcherry, and sumach . . . in undisturbed solitude.
> . . . It is darker, the poet's flute is heard out over the pond and Walden hears the swan song of that "Day" and faintly echoes. . . . 'Tis an evening when the "whole body is one sense," . . . and before ending his day he looks out over the clear, crystalline water of the pond and catches a glimpse of the shadow-thought he saw in the morning's mist and haze. . . . He

goes up the "pleasant hillside of pines, hick-
ories," and moonlight to his cabin, "with a
strange liberty in Nature, a part of herself."

This passage is taken from Ives's *Essays Before a
Sonata*, which the composer wrote because he was not
satisfied to offer only the sonata as his personal tribute
to the Transcendentalists. The essays served partly as an
accompaniment to and partly as an explanation of the
sonata. With his keen sense of humor, which did not
lack a certain seriousness, he wrote in the book's dedication:

These prefatory essays were written by the
composer for those who can't stand his music
—and the music for those who can't stand his
essays; to those who can't stand either, the
whole is respectfully dedicated.

Later on he explained that together the music and
the essays were written to present "one person's impression of the spirit of Transcendentalism that is associated
in the minds of many with Concord, Massachusetts, of
over a half century ago."

The essays are important not only because they help

others understand Ives's music, but also because they give us an understanding of what Ives's *own* spirit was about. When Ives talked about the people of Concord and their qualities, it was almost as if he were talking about himself. For example, a passage about Emerson's method of writing prose is an almost exact description of Ives's method of writing music, particularly the *Concord Sonata*:

> His underlying plan of work seems based on the large unity of a series of particular aspects of a subject, rather than the continuity of its expression. As thoughts surge to his mind, he fills the heavens with them, crowds them in, if necessary, but seldom arranges them along the ground first.

Of course this is a generalization on Ives's part, for we are as sure that Emerson planned out his prose as we are that Ives devised a plan for the Concord Sonata. But because they were both committed to the Transcendental ideal, they were each intent on creating the illusion of an unorganized world of related ideas.

To this day the *Essays* remain highly intelligent, thought-provoking and inspired prose, and the *Concord Sonata* is one of the most beautiful musical works of the

twentieth century. Many years after Ives wrote the sonata, the critic Lawrence Gilman expressed his feeling
for it by proclaiming it "the greatest music composed by
an American."

The *Concord Sonata* was only one of a number of
masterpieces Ives wrote during the years 1906 to 1916.
Some of his most brilliant accomplishments were his
many songs for solo voice and piano, which now hold
a firm place in the body of American art songs.

Ives's volume of *114 Songs* is a treasury of some
of the most unusual and striking works in the entire vocal
repertoire. The texts of the songs come from poems by
famous writers in English, French and German. There
are also religious texts and some poems written by Ives
and his wife Harmony. The styles range from bouncy,
popular tunes to songs that are profoundly serious and
strikingly dissonant.

Although some of the shorter songs like "Serenity,"
"The Greatest Man," "Paracelsus," and "Ann Street"
can be studied as representative works, the magnificent
"General William Booth's Entrance into Heaven," written in 1914, can be considered the culmination of Ives's
song style. Ives's friend and fellow composer Carl Ruggles once said about it:

. . . if Ives never wrote but one song, he would

have been a great composer. That's General
William Booth Enters into Heaven . . . It's a
very great song. It's a song of genius, that's all.

Ives took the text of his song from Vachel Lindsay's
famous poem, which he had seen in a newspaper one day.
It tells of William Booth, the founder of the Salvation
Army, leading his group of wretched souls to heaven
where they find redemption for their sins:

Booth led boldly with his bass drum—
(Are you washed in the blood of the Lamb?)
The Saints smiled gravely and they said: 'He's come.'
(Are you washed in the blood of the Lamb?)
Walking lepers followed, rank on rank,
Lurching bravos from the ditches dank,
Drabs from the alleyways and drug fiends pale—
Minds still passion-ridden, soul-powers frail:—
Vermin-eaten saints with moldy breath,
Unwashed legions with the ways of Death—
(Are you washed in the blood of the Lamb?)

Every slum had sent its half-a-score
The round world over. (Booth had groaned for more.)
Every banner that the wide world flies
Bloomed with glory and transcendent dyes.

76

Big-voiced lasses made their banjos bang,
Tranced, fanatical they shrieked and sang:—
'Are you washed in the blood of the Lamb?'
Hallelujah! It was queer to see
Bull-necked convicts with that land make free.
Loons with trumpets blowed a blare, blare, blare
On, on upward thro' the golden air!
(Are you washed in the blood of the Lamb?)

Jesus came from out the court-house door,
Stretched his hands above the passing poor.
Booth saw not, but led his queer ones there
Round and round the mighty court-house square.
Then, in an instant all that blear review
Marched on spotless, clad in raiment new.
The lame were straightened, withered limbs uncurled
And blind eyes opened on a new, sweet world.

Although Lindsay meant the words to be chanted to
the Salvation Army hymn "Are You Washed in the
Blood of the Lamb?" Ives set the poem to another hymn,
"There Is a Fountain Filled with Blood." The phrase
"Are you washed . . ." returns again and again, almost
like an eighteenth century rondo theme, but in a truly
Ivesian manner it is always in a different harmonic and
rhythmic setting. This is what gives the song its result-

Excerpt from "General William Booth's Entrance Into Heaven," in Ives's hand. PHOTOGRAPH COURTESY JOHN HERRICK JACKSON MUSIC LIBRARY, YALE UNIVERSITY.

ing strength and power. With each return, the hymn tune seems to grow in significance.

Ives's tremendous ability to vary a musical idea creates in this work striking rhythms and harmonies, which combine to make music of tremendous power and drive. The following excerpt in Ives's own hand, shows some of the most powerful measures of the song. The fervor of the procession is recreated every time we come to the passage where the chorus sings and shouts "Hallelujah!" This is its last and most dramatic appearance.

Ives's first sketches for the song were for solo voice and piano, but he later orchestrated the piano part for brass band. Many years later he sent the score to his friend John Becker, who was interested in performing the piece with a chorus and chamber orchestra. Becker's version of the song is performed at least as often today as the original one for voice and piano. The additional instruments and voices intensify the emotions portrayed in the song, and for the feeling of excitement it has few peers in all of American music.

Ives's creative energies seemed to have no limits at this time—he produced an amazing number of important works. Among them are some chamber works: *Tone Roads* and four sonatas for violin and piano among others, and these larger instrumental works: the *Robert Browning Overture*, the *New England Holidays* Symphony and *Three Places in New England*. This orchestral suite consists of musical portraits of the Saint-Gaudens's Memorial in the Boston Commons (Colonel Shaw leading his regiment of black soldiers), Putnam's Camp in Redding, Connecticut, and the Housatonic River at Stockbridge, Massachusetts. The work does not tell a story. Rather it suggests a mood and gives a general impression, in much the same way the *Concord Sonata* leaves us with an impression of the people and spirit of the Transcendentalist movement.

But it is the Fourth Symphony that represents the highest point in Ives's achievement as a composer. It brings to mind something the eminent musician Nicolas Slonimsky said about his friend Charles Ives:

> I don't know how but I understood almost intuitively that there was a great man and that great man was composing great music.

7

The Fourth Symphony

In the summer of 1910, when Ives was 35 years old, he and Harmony decided to make their usual trip up to Elk Lake in the Adirondacks. It was a particularly welcome vacation, for it had come after a rather trying spring of losses among family and friends, sickness and a discouraging rehearsal of Ives's First Symphony with the New York Philharmonic and its unsympathetic conductor Walter Damrosch. Both Charles and Harmony were relieved to be away from the city and were thankful for the peace and solace of their country retreat.

During that summer Ives first began thinking about his Fourth Symphony. Listening to the symphony as it exists in the version completed in 1916, it seems logical that Ives began thinking about it in the country when he was surrounded by the strangely wonderful sounds of the natural world. In fact, some listeners have thought that the organization of some of Ives' music came from the way he saw and heard the world move around him.

When one listens to the Fourth Symphony, one has a vivid impression of passing through a few moments in time—similar to the experience, perhaps, of sitting by the shore of a mountain lake and absorbing the surrounding movements, sounds and sights. One friend of Ives explained the music quite simply as "a photographic replica in sound of a happening." He went on to say, "Everything in him (Ives) is something that he heard happen which he transferred and caught at a moment in time like a photograph."

To achieve these "photographic" musical images, Ives used unusual combinations of instruments that could create sounds never heard before in the concert hall. On the first page of the printed score is a lengthy list of the instruments used during the course of the symphony. There is first the usual assemblage of strings, woodwinds, brass and timpani, but then come the alto, tenor and baritone saxophone, solo piano, orchestral piano for four hands, celeste, organ and a group of percussion instruments including the snare drum, military drum, tom-tom, bass drum, cymbals, bells and gongs. All this plus a full choir of voices! Orchestral works that called for such extensive and unusual gatherings were rare at the time Ives wrote his Fourth Symphony—Mahler's Eighth Symphony and Schoenberg's *Gurrelieder* are among the few other examples. Certainly in America nothing like this had ever been written before.

Even more incredible than the instrumental and vocal forces Ives employed, is the entirely unique way he used them. In all the movements except the third, which is quite traditional, Ives created extremely "modern" musical collages. They are filled with musical images of late nineteenth century America—marching bands, holiday celebrations, hymn singing, popular dance tunes—the sounds of a small New England town like his Danbury. Ives's good friend John Kirkpatrick said that these collages are "like a densely populated landscape or streetscape, or a cloud of hovering angels, or a three-ring circus." The music can be compared to the French composer Claude Debussy's impressionistic orchestral pieces. Ives's music is also impressionistic, but, unlike Debussy's, there is a certain amount of (intentional) disorder and much dissonance. This is what gives the music a distinctly American and modern flavor.

Ives based the Fourth Symphony on the eternal questions man asks of life: "What?" and "Why?". Parts of the symphony were also based on the tune used for the hymn "Watchman, Tell Us of the Night," which for Ives represented the eternal question of man. The night can be thought of as the unknown, as well as man's search for an explanation for our existence, the problem that has troubled man through the ages.

The first movement, the prelude, asks the questions "What?" and "Why?" to the accompaniment of violins and harp in the distance. They play a hymnlike melody that is repeated throughout the movement. The other instruments enter in, and strains of well-known hymns are heard: "In the Sweet Bye and Bye," "I Hear a Welcome Voice," and "Nearer My God to Thee.". This leads up to the entry of the voices, which sing "Watchman, Tell Us of the Night." The melody was one of Ives's favorites; it also occurs in his First Violin Sonata and his song "Watchman."

> Watchman, tell us of the night,
> What the signs of promise are:
> Traveler, o'er yon mountain's height,
> See that Glory-beaming star!
>
> Watchman, aught of joy or hope?
> Traveler, yes; it brings the day,
> Promised day of Israel,
> Dost thou see its beauteous ray?

The second movement, often called the "Comedy," is one of the most original pieces of music ever written. It is the first attempt at answering the questions "What?" and "Why?". The easy way of life and "wordly progress" are contrasted with the grim trials of the Pilgrims, represented in the symphony by excerpts from hymns. According to Ives, the idea for the music was based on a story by Nathaniel Hawthorne (one of the New England Transcendentalists), "The Celestial Railroad."

Someone aptly called the movement an "extraordinary hodgepodge," for within the course of twelve minutes, fragments of more than fifteen popular songs are heard, among them "Tramp, Tramp, Tramp," "In the Sweet Bye and Bye," "The Red, White and Blue," "Beulah Land," "Long, Long Ago," "Reveille," and "The Irish Washerwoman." This is in addition to many others from Ives's own imagination. It is all held together within a framework of three different groups of instruments playing in three different meters which, incidentally, needed three different conductors at its first performance! At one point during the movement more than twenty different rhythms are going at the same time. The score is incredibly complicated; the movement was without a doubt the most complex piece of music written to date.

Ives was fond of this complicated rhythmic effort. But, unfortunately, he was later subject to the criticism that it was unnatural and could not be grasped by normal minds. To this complaint he replied, in his typically

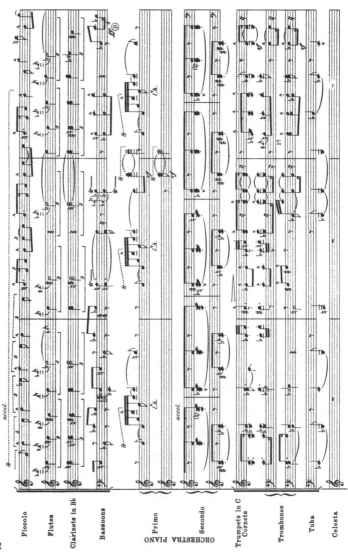

A page of the second movement of the Fourth Symphony showing the simultaneous use of twenty-one different rhythms.

Triangle
High Bells
Low Bells
Tympani High Low
Indian Drum
Snare Drum
Bass Drum
O = with Cym.
Gongs a) Light b) Heavy
Solo Piano
Violins I
Violins II
Violins III
Violas
Violoncellos
Basses

87

humorous manner, with an amazing explanation of how
the rhythms could be easily understood by anyone who
had the patience and will-power to try his method:

> I have with much practice been able to keep
> five, and even six, rhythms going in my mind
> at once, so that I can hear each one naturally
> by leaning toward it, changing the ear in each
> measure. . . . The way I did it was to take, for
> instance, in the left hand a 5—with the left
> foot, beat a 2—with the right foot, beat a 3—
> with the right hand, play an 11—and sing a
> 7. Start with two, gradually add the others—
> perhaps to begin with, have a slow metronome
> with a bell play the one-beat, and think of the
> measure as a 2, then a 3, then a 5, then a 7,
> then an 11. . . . Various other rhythms can be
> held in the mind in this way, and after a while
> they become as natural as it is for Toscanini to
> beat down-left-right-up as evenly as a metro-
> nome for two hours steadily, and do it nice,
> with all the ladies tapping time with their feet.

The rhythms in all of Ives's music were so complex that they often required unusual methods of conducting. Once, during a rehearsal of a passage from
"Washington's Birthday," the conductor Nicolas Slonim-

sky found it necessary to beat in seven with his baton, three with his left hand, and nod his head in two. This no doubt created an amusing sight for performers and audience alike! The conductor Eugene Goosens learned the score of the Fourth Symphony by sitting up nights, wrapping a towel around his head, and drinking gallons of coffee. Conductors today have benefitted from more years' experience with Ives's music, and other music even more complex, so that it poses fewer problems in performance. (Even so, this symphony has had very few performances.)

The totally unconventional music of the second movement of the symphony is in direct contrast to the spirit of traditionalism that the third movement exhibits. For this movement, Ives created a new version for orchestra of the fugue he had used in his First String Quartet, written in 1896.

The third movement was another answer to the eternal questions—it was the "expression of the reaction of life into formalism and ritualism." It is beautiful and stirring music, extremely evocative of Ives's native New England, with its seriousness, tradition and puritanism. Many people have been fond of saying that Ives couldn't write fine "traditional" music—this movement is the proof of the falseness—and irrelevance—of that criticism.

Ives thought the fourth movement of the symphony

one of the finest things he ever wrote, and many would agree. It is a slow "impressionistic landscape" exemplifying the realities of existence and the religious experience of our lives. It is transcendental in the same way the *Concord Sonata* is, for our attention is given to the whole image of the piece rather than to its small details.

Like the first movement, a background group plays its passage throughout this movement; in musical terms this is called an "ostinato." This time the ostinato is provided by a group of percussion instruments—a snare drum, small timpani, cymbal, bass drum and gong. Above this the other instruments move about freely, also quoting, in a subdued fashion, some popular melodies and the hymn "Nearer, My God, to Thee." Toward the end, the choir is heard again, but this time, no words are sung. The chorus hums an interweaving of melodies based on the tune "Bethany," and then fades, until at last we hear only the faint indistinct sounds of the percussion group.

The experience of Ives's Fourth Symphony is too fascinating, deep and moving to be explained in words. It must be listened to. It takes several hearings to comprehend its complete originality and unmistakeable Americanism. And if we venture to read a bit of Ives's beloved *Walden*, we can understand how much truth there was in Thoreau's words:

. . . Let every one mind his own business, and endeavor to be what he has made. . . . If a man does not keep pace with his companions, perhaps it is because he hears a different drummer. Let him step to the music which he hears, however measured or far away.

8

Ives's Retirement from Music: The Beginnings of an Audience

Ives's most highly creative and prolific period of writing music lasted about 15 years. It ended in 1916. After that his music did not flow as easily as it had before. One day in 1926 he walked into the room where his wife was sitting and told her sadly that he couldn't seem to write music any more. He seemed finally to have used himself up.

There were a number of reasons for this. For one thing, when the United States entered the First World War in 1917, Ives became too concerned with the war to write much music. Although he did not read newspapers often and did not actually follow political events closely, he was constantly preoccupied with the moral and political questions that arose from the war, and for that matter, from all wars. For all of his life he maintained the highest ideals about justice for all people. He was an ardent pacifist who believed that the strong national patriotism of people led to nonsensical conflicts, as was clearly evident in the First World War.

But at the same time, when the United States joined the Allies in 1917, Ives became so excited about it that his activities concerned with the war effort took up a great deal of what was normally his composing time, and also exhausted his emotional energy. Probably he, like many other people, thought this would be "the war to end all wars," and in his own way he wanted to do as much as he could to assure victory for the Allies. At first he wanted to join the Red Cross and drive an ambulance abroad, but his health was not good enough. So as a substitute for active participation, he worked at the sale of U.S. Liberty Bonds, by which citizens could invest in the war effort. In June of 1917, he and Julian Myrick gave their employees two days off so they could sell Liberty Bonds. Ives also donated two fully equipped ambulances to the United States Army.

Since his health was not good, and he was so concerned with other things, working at his music became extremely difficult. In October of 1918, he had a severe physical breakdown, and for the rest of his life he suf-

93

fered from heart disease, diabetes and cataracts. (In spite
of this, however, he lived to the age of seventy-nine.)

His emotional involvement in the war and the political state of the country obviously did not help his
health. One relative of Ives told the story of an extraordinary meeting of a committee set up to establish and
sell Liberty Bonds. Franklin Roosevelt was a member,
and so was Ives.

> Charlie thought that there ought to be a small
> fifty-dollar bond so that everybody could con-
> tribute and be part of it. Franklin Roosevelt
> . . . scorned the idea of anything so useless as
> a fifty-dollar bond. Charlie had an argument
> with him and Charlie won, but he had a heart
> attack either during or directly after the meet-
> ing. . . . It was so bad that they couldn't move
> him from the hotel.

We cannot be entirely certain that FDR was the one
Ives argued with at the meeting—but whether he was
or not, the point of the story stands. Ives was passion-
ate in his belief that the common man should be given
a voice.

About this time he was writing articles like "The
Majority" (also the title of one of his songs), and a pro-

posal for a twentieth amendment to the U.S. Constitution. Ives's proposal suggested that American citizens should not only have a direct say in deciding who should govern, but should also be able to vote on actual issues. He was extremely serious about this proposed amendment, and sent copies of it not only to major newspapers and magazines, but also to President Woodrow Wilson and other prominent political figures like Calvin Coolidge, Herbert Hoover, William Jennings Bryan and William Taft. The responses were generally negative, and Ives was extremely disappointed in this. It only proved to him even more how little one man's ideas meant to the country and those who ran it.

One of the few pieces of music he wrote during the war exhibits the strength of his beliefs. The words of the song "They Are There," written in 1917, are the composer's own:

When we're through this cursed war,
All started by a sneaking gouger, making slaves of men,
Then let all the people rise
And stand together in brave, kind
     Humanity.
Most wars are made by small, stupid,
     selfish, bossing groups.
While the people have no say.

But there'll come a day—hip hip
    hooray!—
When they'll smash all dictators
    to the wall.
Then it's build a people's world
    nation—hooray!
Ev'ry honest country's free to live
    its own native life.
They will stand for the right,
But if it comes to might
They are there, they are there,
    they are there!
Then the people, not just politicians,
Will rule their own lands and lives.
Then you'll hear the whole universe shouting
    the battle cry of Freedom.
Tenting on a new camp ground.
Tenting tonight,
Tenting on a new camp ground.
For it's rally 'round the flag of the
    people's free new world,
Shouting the battle cry of Freedom.

The song was not a great success, not only because
of the words, but also because the music lacked the strong
sense of "rightness" that his music had always had. Most
things he wrote or attempted to write in the war years

and after lacked the inner life that had made his earlier works so great. Perhaps he had become so involved in causes that he was trying to make music serve a cause rather than itself, and this is part of the reason he had so much trouble composing.

The irony in Ives's career is that only after he stopped composing did his music begin to be recognized by people outside his immediate circle. This process of recognition was painfully long and slow, and his acceptance of it even slower, because he had to make up for all the years when people had done nothing but criticize.

Incidents of people criticizing his music were well-embedded in Ives's mind. Typical of these was the visit of a well-known violinist who, when he played the First Violin Sonata, was reported to have said;

"This cannot be played. It is awful. It is not music, it makes no sense . . . when you get awfully indigestible food in your stomach that distresses you, you can get rid of it, but I cannot get those horrible sounds out of my ears."

A comment about the "Fourth of July" from the *New England Holidays* Symphony went like this: "That's the best joke I've seen for a long time. Do you really think anybody would be fool enough to try to play a thing like that?" Even people Ives considered to be friends were relentless in their attacks on his music. One friend, after hearing one of Ives's pieces, exclaimed ". . . How CAN you like horrible sounds like that?"

One of the earliest performances of Ives's music gives an example of the typical reaction. In March of 1910, Walter Damrosch, the famous conductor of the New York Philharmonic, had been persuaded by a friend of Ives to try out one of the composer's compositions. Damrosch was, as might be expected for a man in his position at that time, quite conservative in his views about music. Like Horatio Parker, he was a fine musician, but no great lover of new musical ideas.

So at one of the regular Saturday morning rehearsals, parts of Ives's First Symphony, which he had written at Yale, were distributed to the Philharmonic musicians. Ives described part of the scene:

> . . . He (Damrosch) started with the second movement (adagio), an English horn tune over chords in the strings. When he heard the pretty little theme and nice chords he called out "charming!" When the second themes got going together, and the music got a little more involved (but not very involved), he acted somewhat put out, got mad, and said it

couldn't be played without a great deal of re-
hearsing.

But Damrosch went on, often stopping to correct
what he assumed were wrong notes, but which the composer had actually written as intentionally as the "pretty
little theme and nice chords." At one point the rhythm
became a little bit complex, using the device of two
against three—which Chopin, Brahms and even Beethoven had used—and Damrosch turned around to the
composer and snapped, "You'll just have to make up
your mind, young man! Which do you want, a rhythm
of two or a rhythm of three?"

Ives never forgot this experience, or Damrosch's
unwillingness to consider anything that was out of the
ordinary. Consequently, the famous conductor became
one of the group of established musicians that Ives constantly made jokes about, especially after he became
famous.

A similar event was described by Ives's nephew
Brewster, who often came from Danbury, where his
father had a law practice, to visit Uncle Charles and Aunt
Harmony in the city. Ives took his nephew, of whom
he was quite fond, to hear a concert at the old Aeolian
Hall on West 43rd Street, where one of his violin sonatas
was being played. According to Brewster, as soon as the

audience heard the unfamiliar, dissonant sounds of the sonata, they began to make comments that eventually became louder and louder until some people just shouted their dislike and walked out of the room. Ives got up and turned to his nephew saying, "I think we'd better go home."

Even though Ives became famous in his later years —so famous, in fact, that he gave up his daily walks around his block on East 74th Street because people stopped him on the street—he never quite got rid of the memory of the bitter disappointments he had suffered earlier. Because of that, he became almost cynical about his fame when it came. He was not interested in hearing other people's comments about his music. The music had been written because it was right for him, not because he had wanted to please others.

Perhaps this hardness that Ives maintained throughout his life came out of his traditional New England upbringing. Other great New Englanders—Emerson, Thoreau and Emily Dickinson—had had this sternness about their work and would not accept criticism from anyone. These people had, in fact, been respected for their firmness and integrity.

One of the people who understood and praised Ives for his personal strength was the great Austrian composer, Arnold Schoenberg. Schoenberg and Ives, though contemporaries, were not too familiar with each other's work, and unfortunately never met. But toward the end of their lives, they each learned a bit about the other. After Schoenberg's death in America, his wife found a paper on his desk on which he had written the following tribute:

> There is a great man living in this Country—
>   a composer.
> He has solved the problem how to preserve
>   one's self and to learn.
> He responds to negligence by contempt.
> He is not forced to accept praise or blame.
> His name is Ives.

Part of the reason Schoenberg felt so strongly about Ives's situation as an unpopular composer was that he had also suffered under criticism. Like Ives, he had known all along that what he was doing in music was right, and he refused to let other people disturb his work with their constant attacks.

Ives was enthusiastic about his music during the time he was writing well, and in all the years after. Though at first he had little support, it would be unfair to say he had none. There were always a few people who were open-minded enough to see that Ives was writing some fine music. One of these people was Gustav Mahler, who had been impressed with the Third Symphony.

Another positive response in the earlier years came from the violinist David Talmadge who played Ives's violin sonatas for him. According to Ives, he "gave them serious, hard and intelligent study, and played them well and in a kind of big way."

But aside from these people—and a few others, like the conductor Edgar Stowell, who were enthusiastic about those works that were not as "modern" and dissonant as some others—few people knew or accepted Ives and his work. Then in about 1921 he decided to publish, at his own expense, his *Concord Sonata*, the *Essays Before a Sonata*, and a collection of some of his finest vocal music, *114 Songs*. Up to that time none of his music had appeared in print.

He sent the printed volumes, free, to friends, musicians, critics and libraries. Very likely, most of the copies were thrown in the wastebasket. But the few people who had the patience to sit down and devote some time to the books realized that there was an unmistakable cleverness and wit in the writings, and an unquestionable musical genius in the Sonata and the Songs.

One of the people fortunate enough to discover Ives through the publications was a well-known Southern poet and journalist, Henry Bellamann. As a direct result of these publications, Bellamann became a promoter of Ives's music. His first effort was a review of the *Concord Sonata* in a New Orleans newspaper. This was in 1921. Within a few months he had arranged some public lectures about Ives, where he had a pianist friend play some excerpts from the sonata. His wife Katherine sang some of the songs.

The reaction of the public to Bellamann's lecture–recitals was mixed. Most of the people felt that it was all too new and difficult to understand. Others simply didn't like it, as evidenced by the headline of a newspaper review—"A Terribly Hard Taste of Music." Yet because of the lectures, more people had heard about Ives.

The word spread slowly, but it did spread. One incident that helped was a totally coincidental meeting that took place in 1924. A French pianist named E. Robert Schmitz, who had studied at the Paris Conservatory and had known the great French composer Claude Debussy, was ushered into Ives's private room at the large offices of Ives and Myrick. He sat down expecting to talk about an insurance policy for himself and was surprised and intrigued to find himself talking to a composer. Within a short time the two men had become good friends, and Schmitz was convinced that Ives music was worth doing something about in a serious way.

Schmitz was the founder of an organization called Pro Musica, which was primarily concerned with the performance of contemporary music. With his help, some concerts with music by Ives were set up and some of his music was printed in the *Pro Musica Quarterly* .

In 1927 Schmitz helped to launch the first really important performance of an Ives work. His organization had conducted a survey to discover what relatively unknown contemporary composer people were most curious about. One of the composers chosen was Ives, and it was decided that two movements from his Fourth Symphony would be played in a concert that also included music by Debussy and Darius Milhaud, a French composer who lived in the United States for a good part of his life. The concert was conducted by the well-known Eugene Goossens, and the program notes were written by Henry Bellamann.

Although the audience was not entirely enthusiastic about Ives's music, there were some positive reactions. One was from Darius Milhaud. Milhaud, who unlike Ives, was a fairly well-established composer in the public's eye, told Schmitz that he was impressed by the ideas in Ives's music, many of which he had never encountered anywhere before.

The newspaper critics seem to have discovered something at the concert, too. Olin Downes wrote in the *New York Times*:

This writer records that his preference among the new works of the afternoon was for the music of Mr. Ives. The music is not nearly as compact, as finished in workmanship, as smart in tone, as that of Mr. Milhaud, but it rings truer, it seems to have something more genuine behind it. . . .

There is something in this music; real vitality, real naivete, and a superb self-respect. . . . There is the conviction of a composer who dares to jump with feet and hands and a reckless somersault or two on his way to his destination.

What impressed Downes most was the spontaneous Americanism of Ives's music—something he and the other listeners had not heard before in the music of their countrymen.

9

New Friends

At about the time of the Pro Musica concert, Charles and Harmony and their daughter Edith had moved to a lovely three-story brownstone house on East 74th Street in New York City. In the years that followed, the house suited their rather quiet life style well. Quiet, that is, except when Ives burst into one of his periodic rages against the people who didn't understand his music—"sissy" musicians who couldn't grasp what was behind the strong sounds. For as his music began to be heard and began to make friends, it also found more critics. Luckily, Harmony was usually there to check her husband's excitements. Her soothing voice and calm disposition worked well in putting Charles out of his rages, and he was able to resume talking about music with his friends in a rational manner.

One of Ives's new friends, Henry Cowell, was the first really distinguished musician he had come to know well. Cowell, a California-born composer more than twenty years Ives's junior, met Ives in 1927. He got to know Ives's music, and once past the surface difficulties, realized, as no one had before, that Ives was the true father of American music. Cowell was to become Ives's staunchest supporter over the next thirty years, and also his first biographer. Because Cowell was also a composer, unlike Schmitz or Bellamann, he could sympathize completely with Ives. He was going through similar problems in composing music that was essentially unpopular.

Discovering Ives was a revelation for Cowell, and he quickly spread the new music around to his friends— a group of composers now referred to as the American Experimentalists. Among these people were Ruth Crawford Seeger, Carl Ruggles, Wallingford Riegger, John Becker and Otto Luening. Most of them had been composing music that was distinctly American long before they knew Ives. But learning about Ives's music and career gave them a new confidence in their own work. They saw that Ives had insisted upon writing music the way he wanted to, even if others thought it wasn't right. And they found ideas in his music that they had also used or could learn from: polytonality, quarter tones, complex rhythms, new instrumental sounds and the concept of organizing music into conglomerates of complex sounds.

Henry Cowell was the founder and editor of the

periodical *New Music*, which helped composers and musicians keep up with new trends in the music world. The publication printed new scores, and in 1929 it offered the second movement of Ives's Fourth Symphony. It was one of the most ambitious projects the magazine had undertaken because the score was so extremely complex.

The following year Cowell introduced Ives to a young Russian-born conductor and composer, Nicolas Slonimsky. Today Slonimsky is known as one of the great promoters of American music, but at that time he was only beginning to discover what riches the American musical scene had to offer. He had heard of Ives's music, but the meeting reinforced his desire to conduct some of it. In January 1931 he put together a performance with his Boston Chamber Orchestra of *Three Places in New England*. Ives, who had now retired because of his poor health and was living off the healthy profits of his insurance business, helped to fund the concert. This was the beginning of a period covering twenty years, when he was one of the chief sources of funds for concerts and publications of twentieth century music, including his own.

The performance of *Three Places in New England* was also given in New York at Town Hall. One of the other pieces on the program was Carl Ruggles's masterful *Men and Mountains*, an orchestral work of great intensity. People at the concert were a bit surprised when they saw a man—Charles Ives—rise from his seat and shout to a young man who was reacting to Ruggles's music rather noisily, "Stop being such a God-damned sissy! Why can't you stand up before fine strong music like this and use your ears like a man!"

Soon after the Boston and New York concerts, Henry Cowell decided that Europe might be a good place to introduce American symphonic music; and when he discussed a plan for some concerts with Ives and Slonimsky, the two were more than eager to participate—Ives by funding the concerts and Slonimsky by conducting them. For some reason Europeans have always been more impressed than Americans with American music. They have been more able to listen to the music objectively and forget about certain inborn prejudices. This is still true today; many American jazz musicians, unknown in their own country, are acclaimed as true artists across the Atlantic. And so it was for Ives, Cowell, Ruggles and the other composers represented on the Pan-American concerts that Slonimsky conducted in Europe. The European critics offered lofty praise for the music, and the audiences, though not ecstatic, were impressed with the spontaneity and warmth of the pieces.

But feelings back home were in no way similar. Word of the concerts got around, and some American newspapers carried violent critiques of the Slonimsky concerts. Philip Hale, the music critic of the *Boston Globe*, not knowing much more about the composers and the music than what he read on the printed program which had been sent to him, submitted a scathing editorial to the paper. In it he made sweeping judgements of the music, based largely on what he had heard in passing from others who had some familiarity with it. Hale wrote:

Nicolas Slonimsky of Boston, indefatigable in furthering the cause of the extreme radical composers, has brought out in Paris orchestral compositions by Americans who are looked on by our conservatives as wild-eyed anarchists. He thus purposed to acquaint Parisians with contemporaneous American music. But the composers represented were not those who are regarded by their fellow-countrymen as leaders in the art, nor have they all been so considered by the conductors of our great orchestras. If Mr. Slonimsky had chosen a composition by Loeffler, Hill, one of Deems Taylor's suites, Foote's suite, or music by some who, working along traditional lines, have nevertheless shown taste, technical skill and a suggestion at least of individuality, his audiences in Paris would now have a fairer idea of what Americans are doing in their art.

It was true that the four composers Hale mentioned were better-known in America, and they did have the support of the established conductors and orchestras. But the irony of his comments is that these four composers are not very well known today. Where Ives, Cowell, Ruggles, Riegger and Varese are now established names in music, Loeffler, Hill, Taylor and Foote are almost completely forgotten.

In discussing the concerts further, Hale implied that the Americans had been influenced by the "radical" European composers—Stravinsky, Prokofieff, Hindemith—three of the finest and most celebrated composers of the century.

Are these Parisians to be blamed if they say that the American composers thus made known to them are restless experimenters, or followers of Europeans whose position in the musical world is not yet determined, men who show ingenuity chiefly by their rhythmic inventions and orchestral tricks; men who apparently have no melodic gift, having it, disdain it for the tiresome repetition and transfor-

mation of an insignificant pattern; who neglect
the sensuous charm of stringed instruments
and put their trust for startling effects in combinations of wind and percussion choirs; followers, but with unequal footsteps, of Stravinsky, Prokofieff and certain continental composers of whom Hindemith is a promient example?

Naturally, there was a mixture of anger and disbe-
lief among the composers who had been slandered in
Hale's editorial. They could not believe that a man whose
knowledge of the music was so narrow could have the
audacity to print such extreme comments. Ives was certainly outraged.

The day after he received a clipping of Hale's editorial in the mail, he decided to go ahead with composing
some autobiographical notes, which his friends had been
urging him to do. These *Memos*, since their recent publication, have become an invaluable source for all who
have studied Ives and his music. They are perfectly frank
in their analyses of people like Hale, who did not have
the strength, as Ives put it, to listen to new sounds.

What infuriated Ives most about Hale's article was
the insinuation that he was a follower of Hindemith and
similar composers. In the *Memos* Ives pointed out that

not only had he never heard a note of Hindemith's music, but that he had written all of his works (and particularly the *New England Holidays* symphony that was played at the Pan-American concerts) before Hindemith even started his composing career.

The *New York Times* offered a review of Pan-American concerts that was equal to Hale's in its tone. But at least it was written by someone who had attended the concerts—a French critic named Henry Prunières. Much to Slonimsky's and Ives's dismay the *Times* had picked almost the only European critic who had reacted unfavorably to the music to write the review. Like Hale, Prunières falsely accused the composers of being followers of Europeans and openly stated that Ives had gotten some of his ideas from Schoenberg. This was as ridiculous as the comment about Hindemith, and Ives launched back in his own humorous way:

> He [Prunières] says that I know my Schoenberg—interesting information to me, as I have never heard nor seen a note of Schoenberg's music. Then he says that I haven't "applied the lessons as well as I might." This statement shows almost human intelligence. It's funny how many men, when they see another man put the "breechin'" under a horse's tail, wrong

or right, think that he must be influenced by someone in Siberia or Neurasthenia. No one man invented the barber's itch.

But as much as the accusations of the critics hurt Ives and the others in his group, they realized that it was better to have one's music hated than to have it unnoticed. And they were pleased to note that their strange new sounds were causing a stir among the concert-going public; in spite of themselves, people were becoming interested.

10

A Great
American Composer

After fifty years, Ives was beginning to get his reward. More than a handful of people had taken notice of him. A considerable number of people seemed to have heard some intriguing new sounds and been stirred by their genuineness and stark beauty. The music had even led a few of them to pick up one of the surviving copies of the 1920 printing of "Essay Before a Sonata" and they had been fascinated and moved by its contents. One passage of the Prologue stood out among the rest:

> . . . we would rather believe that music is beyond any analogy to word language and that the time is coming, but not in our lifetime, when it will develop possibilities unconceivable now—a language, so transcendent, that its

heights and depths will be common to all mankind.

These words made more sense to people in the late 1930s than they had in 1920. Listeners were beginning to realize that what they heard in Ives's music was, if not a truly universal musical language, one that was striving to achieve it. Many found something in the music that touched them in a most personal way—a tune they had sung as a child, a memory of a marching band playing for a holiday celebration, a snatch of some dance rhythm, or a few bars of a ragtime melody. All those elements combined into creating a musical atmosphere that was transcendental—that gave them something deeper than a concord of pleasant sounds.

It was at a concert in New York in 1939 that people seemed to finally grasp the depth in Ives's music. Many were people who had become interested in the music before for its strikingly original sounds and uncommon forms. But these were only the surface qualities of the music. Audiences had never really been moved by the quality that Ives had tried hardest to instill in his music, the universal—or transcendental—spirit.

The landmark concert that seemed to awaken people to the real Ives with the first complete public performance of the *Concord Sonata*. It was given in January of 1939 in New York City's Town Hall by a young

JOHN
KIRKPATRICK
Piano Recital

TOWN HALL
113 West 43rd Street

FRIDAY EVENING AT 8:30
JANUARY 20th

Sonata in C major, Op. 53   BEETHOVEN
I. allegro con brio
II. Introduzione, adagio molto
Rondo, allegretto moderato—prestissimo

Concord, Mass., 1840-60   CHARLES E. IVES
SECOND PIANOFORTE SONATA (1911-15)
("an attempt to present one person's impression of the spirit of transcendentalism that
is associated in the minds of many with Concord, Mass., of over a half century ago")

I. Emerson   ("a composite picture or impression")

II. Hawthorne (an "extended fragment" reflecting "some of his wilder, fantastical
adventures into the half-childlike, half-fairylike phantasmal realms")

III. The Alcotts ("a sketch")

IV. Thoreau ("an autumn day of Indian summer at Walden")

FIRST PERFORMANCE

STEINWAY PIANO

Tickets: Box seats $2.75, Orchestra $2.20, $1.65, $1.10, Balcony $.83
Tax included   At Box Office

Management RICHARD COPLEY, Steinway Bldg., 113 West 57th St., New York, N. Y.

The program of John Kirkpatrick's landmark concert of the
Concord Sonata. PHOTOGRAPH COURTESY JOHN HERRICK JACK-
SON MUSIC LIBRARY, YALE UNIVERSITY.

117

pianist named John Kirkpatrick. Kirkpatrick had first seen the score of the sonata at a friend's house in Paris, and he was intrigued with it from the outset. He spent the next ten years studying it off and on, writing to Ives and going over parts of it with him, giving performances of separate movements occasionally. Then in 1939 he finally felt he understood the music well enough to present it in its entirety at a major concert hall.

The ten years of study had their reward, for the concert was an unprecedented success. The audience was struck with the power and sensitivity of the music, made clear by the profound understanding of the interpreter. Kirkpatrick was even forced by their applause to repeat one movement.

The next day an article appeared in the New York *Herald Tribune*, reporting that an historic event had taken place in Town Hall. Lawrence Gilman's review of Kirkpatrick's concert proclaimed Ives "the most original and extraordinary of American composers" and went on to register his feelings about the sonata:

> This sonata is exceptionally great music—
> it is indeed the greatest music composed by an
> American, and the most deeply and essentially
> American in impulse and implication. It is wide
> ranging and capacious. It has passion, tender-

ness, humor, simplicity, homeliness. It has wisdom and beauty and profundity, and a sense of the encompassing terror and splendor of human life and human destiny—a sense of those mysteries that are both human and divine.

The public reacted so favorably to the music that a second performance was scheduled in February, and Kirkpatrick was persuaded to play the sonata at concerts in his upcoming tour around the country. Everywhere the audiences continued to be enthusiastic.

Even though he kept getting good reports on Kirkpatrick's concerts, Ives remained cool. He was pleased with his new fame, but it did not go to his head. The disappointments and frustrations of earlier years could not be forgotten, and they cast a shadow over the present. But still, it did seem strange to remember what he thought in some anxious moments twenty years before:

Why is it I like to use these different things and try out other ways . . . which nobody else evidently has any pleasure in hearing, seeing and thinking about? Why do I like to do it? Is there some peculiar defect in me, or something worse that I'm afflicted with?

Everything that was happening made these comments more ironic. The Kirkpatrick concert was like the rock that starts an avalanche. Concerts of Ives's music and articles about him began to appear all over. There were a few retrospective concerts of the music in Los Angeles (with music of Ives's exact contemporary, Arnold Schoenberg), performances of some of the songs in New York, and a recital of the Fourth Violin Sonata by one of the foremost violinists of the day, Joseph Szigeti. The composers Elliott Carter and Aaron Copland and the critics Olin Downes and Paul Rosenfeld all offered important articles on Ives in leading periodicals.

Recordings of Ives's music were also made, among them: Nicolas Slonimsky conducting part of the *New England Holidays*; John Kirkpatrick playing the *Concord Sonata*; Joseph Szigeti playing the Fourth Violin Sonata; and Lehman Engel conducting the "67th Psalm."

The American cultural establishment began to notice Ives, too. In 1946 he was elected to the National Institute of Arts and Letters, a widely respected and distinguished organization of writers, artists and musicians. A year later Ives was awarded the highest honor an American composer can receive, the Pulitzer Prize, for his Third Symphony. This was given after a performance conducted by the composer Lou Harrison.

Most composers would have treasured the Pulitzer Prize, but Ives shrugged his shoulders over it. He replied to the committee that had awarded it to him, "Prizes are for boys. I'm grown-up," and proceeded to give away the five hundred dollars he received. Ives could hardly be blamed for his attitude. Why should he feel excited about a prize for a piece of music he had written forty-three years before? After receiving the prize he wrote to Lou Harrison:

Dear Lou Harry Son

Mr. Ives says: "as you are very much to blame for getting me in to that Pulitzer Prize Street, and for having a bushel of letters to answer and for having a check of $500 thrown at me by the trustees of Colum–Uni– you have to help me by taking ½ of this (somewhere enclosed), and the rest I'll send to the New Music Edition and Arrow Press . . ."

You probably know that Mr. Ives thinks no man in his 73rd year should take every thing very seriously, so I let him dictate this first paragraph. However we both do feel that if you (had) not done so much in behalf of the "3rd" this prize might have gone to Vickey Herbert et al.

It was not just the years of nonrecognition that had left Ives relatively unexcited about his newfound fame. There was a deeper reason, something in his personality, largely molded by his firm, Puritan upbringing. Ives believed strongly that fame was unimportant, and that no one should receive special treatment or favor above anyone else.

Certainly, there are many simple and humble people in the world, but it is not often that famous people fall within their ranks. Ives was unique. He was not only a great musician, but also a man of rare integrity, whose feeling for his fellow human beings reached heights of true greatness.

His friends knew how humble he was. His retirement from the insurance business had left him a millionaire, but he chose not to live like one. He gave a good part of the profits back to the company, and it helped assure the firm of the continuing success that it enjoyed for twenty years.

Ives had also given a lot of money to pay for concerts and publication of new music. Now that he was becoming well known, publishers were interested in bringing out more of his music; when they contacted Ives, they received a surprising reply. He was perfectly willing for them to go ahead with the printing, but he insisted on meeting all of the costs himself. He did not want the music used for any money-making purpose. He also asked that it not be copyrighted. When his Fourth Symphony was accidentally copyrighted by its publisher, Ives angrily responded:

> Everybody who wants a copy is to have one! If anyone wants to copy or reprint these pieces, that's fine! This music is not to make money but to be known and heard. Why should I interfere with its life by hanging on to some sort of personal legal right in it?

At first people thought this a rather bizarre idea; but as they became more familiar with Ives, they began to respect him for his humanitarian ideals.

During the later years of his life, Charles and Harmony spent more and more time at their fourteen acre farm in West Redding, Connecticut. He liked being in those hills near Danbury where he had hiked and camped as a young man. There were frequent visitors to the house —Henry Cowell, Carl Ruggles, Nicolas Slonimsky and John Kirkpatrick among them. Whenever they came, they were struck with the peace of the place; and when they left, it was with a renewed confidence in themselves and their pursuits in the music world.

Nicolas Slonimsky: "You know, one rather friendly individual asked Ives why he wouldn't compose something people would like to hear. He said, 'I can't. I hear something different.'"
PHOTOGRAPH COURTESY JOHN HERRICK JACKSON MUSIC LIBRARY, YALE UNIVERSITY.

In all the years the Iveses owned the large but modest house and surrounding land, there were few changes. They lived in a simple way, with few, if any, of the modern conveniences and luxuries. Ives didn't even have a phonograph to hear the new recordings of his music that were being made and sent to him. What he and Harmony most enjoyed was the serenity of the countryside. Ives never grew tired of the natural world, and in it he found a deep religious inspiration. He had once set a poem by John Greenleaf Whittier to music; its words reflected his feelings.

Serenity

O Sabbath rest of Galilee!
O calm of hills above
Where Jesus knelt to share with thee
The silence of eternity
Interpreted by love.

Drop thy still dews of quietness
Till all our strivings cease
Take from our souls the strain and stress
And let our ordered lives confess
The beauty of thy peace.

At the farm in West Redding, Ives also found himself thinking occasionally about his *Universe Symphony*, a project he had begun back in the twenties. This he had intended to be:

> . . . a contemplation in tones, rather than in music as such, of the mysterious creation of the earth and firmament, the evolution of all life in nature and in humanity to the Divine.

He had planned from the beginning that the symphony would remain unfinished because it was to mirror life, which is constantly changing and never ending. He had even invited other composers to share in its composition, in order to increase the "universal" aspect of the symphony. But the symphony never progressed beyond numerous sketches and a general plan of its contents, which read:

Plan for a Universe Symphony

1. Formation of the countries and mountains
2. Evolution in nature and humanity
3. The rise of all to the spiritual

Occasionally he would add a note here and there on the sketches, and then he would go back to the barn where he kept hundreds of pages of manuscript of other pieces, stored in some old cabinets. He knew that many

of the manuscripts to his pieces were in an almost un-
readable state, but he lacked the energy and the interest
to sit down and try to organize everything. He was always thinking of the larger problem—how the music
was going to reach people. He was still preoccupied with
the transcendentalist ideal, and remembered a few lines
he had written years ago:

> The future of music may not be with music
> itself, but rather . . . in the way it makes itself
> a part with the finer things humanity does and
> dreams of.

Charles Ives died quietly on May 19, 1954, in New
York City. His funeral was attended by a few close
friends and his family. One of the friends, the pianist
John Kirkpatrick, wrote to the composer Carl Ruggles
and his wife about the serenity of Ives's last hours, as
they had been described to Kirpatrick by Mrs. Ives. In
ending his letter he said something about Ives's music
that can be appreciated by all those who have come to
realize its greatness:

> But let us thank God for its core of un-
> shakeable reality, so warmly human, so sure
> in form, so high in impulse. What a great ex-
> ample!

Afterword

The number of performances, recordings, articles, books and lectures on Ives that have appeared since his death in 1954 is too long to list here. Every year the activities have increased and so have our understanding and appreciation of this eccentric and wonderful New England composer and his music.

Especially now that his one hundredth birthday is past and interest in American music has truly blossomed, the name of Ives has become almost as familiar to Americans as Emily Dickinson, Henry David Thoreau and Mark Twain. Ives would have chuckled over that, telling himself it couldn't really be true. That, after all, is part of the essence of his New England spirit.

Suggestions
For Further Reading

Books about and by Charles Ives

Charles Ives and His Music, by Henry and Sidney Cowell (Oxford, 1955, rev. 1969)

This is a complete biography of Ives. Written by the composer Henry Cowell and his wife, who were among Ives's closest friends, it contains a detailed account of Ives's life and explains the most significant aspects of his music.

Charles Edward Ives: Memos, ed. by John Kirkpatrick (Norton, 1972)

John Kirkpatrick, the noted Ives scholar, spent many years assembling all the manuscripts and miscellaneous writings of the composer. This is a collection of all the autobiographical writings, with accompanying annotations. It contains a wealth of previously unpublished information about Ives's life.

Charles Ives Remembered, by Vivian Perlis
    (Yale, 1974)
    The author of this book spent five years interviewing people who knew Ives and worked with him—friends, relatives, business acquaintances and musicians. The portrait that emerges from these published interviews is extraordinarily valuable in understanding Ives both as a person and as a musician.

Essays Before a Sonata and Other Writings, by Charles Ives. ed. by Howard Boatwright (Norton, 1962).

Books about American Music

America's Music, by Gilbert Chase, 2nd. edition (McGraw Hill, 1966)

Music In the United States: A Historical Introduction, by H. Wiley Hitchcock, 2nd. edition (Prentice-Hall, 1974)

Our American Music, by John Tasker Howard, 4th edition (Crowell, 1965)

The New Music, by Aaron Copland (Norton, 1968)

Summary
of The Principal Works
# of Charles Ives

with some suggested recordings

Orchestral Works

Symphony No. 1 in D minor (1896-1898)
  Gould, Chicago Symphony, RCA LSC 2893

Symphony No. 2 (1897-1909)
  Hermann, London Symphony, Lon. 21086

Symphony No. 3 (1904-1909)
  Bernstein, N. Y. Philharmonic, Col. MS-6843

Symphony No. 4 (1910-1916)
  Stokowski, American Symphony Orch., Col. MS-6775

Three Places in New England (1903-1914)
  Thomas, Boston Symphony, DG 2530048

Symphony, "New England Holidays" (1914-1913)
Bernstein, N. Y. Philharmonic, Col. MS-7147

Robert Browning Overture (1908-1912)
Strickland, Polish National Radio Orchestra, CRI 196

The Unanswered Question (1906)
Gould, Chicago Symphony, RCA LSC 2893

Universe Symphony (unfinished) (1911-1928)

Vocal Music

Three Harvest Home Chorales (1898-1912)
Gregg Smith Singers, Col. MS 6921

12 Psalms for Mixed Choir
Gregg Smith Singers, Col. MS 7321

Over 150 songs for solo voice with piano
Selections:
Evelyn Lear & Thomas Stewart, Col. M 30229
Helen Boatwright, 4 Col. M4 32504
Gregg Smith Singers, Col. MS 6921

Chamber Music

String Quartet No. 1 (1896) & No. 2 (1907-1913)
Juilliard Quartet, Col. MS 7027

Sonatas Nos. 1 - 4 for violin and piano (1902-1914)
    Paul Zukofsky and Gilbert Kalish, 2 None. 73025

Solo Instrumental Music

Piano Sonata No. 1 (1902-1910)
    William Masselos, Odys. 3216005-9

Piano Sonata No. 2 "Concord" (1909-1915)
    John Kirkpatrick, Col. MS 7192

numerous works for organ (anthems, hymns, psalms, marches, fugues and variations)

Index

American Experimentalists, 107
Americanism in Ives's music, 105, 118–119
antiphonal effects, 16, 17
"Autumn Landscape from Pine Mountain," 58

Bach, Johann Sebastian, 19, 43
Becker, John, 79, 107
Bellamann, Henry, 103, 104
"The Bells of Yale," 33
Berg, Alban, 66
Boston Chamber Orchestra, 108
Boston Globe review, 110–112
Buck, Dudley, 24

The Celestial Country, 46–47
Clemens, Samuel (see Twain, Mark)
Concord Sonata, 58, 59, 66, 68–75, 80, 90, 102, 103, 116–119, 120
Cowell, Henry, 25, 67, 107, 108, 109, 111, 123

Damrosch, Walter, 81, 98–99
Debussy, Claude, xiii, 83, 103, 104
d'Indy, Vincent, 29
dissonance, 48–49, 50, 67, 83, 100
Downes, Olin, 104–105, 120

"ear-stretching," 12–13, 49
Elk Lake, 58, 60, 81
Emerson, Ralph Waldo, 15, 16, 67, 71, 74, 100
    "Self Reliance," 15, 16

137

Engel, Lehman, 120
Essays Before a Sonata, 73, 74, 102, 115–116

First String Quartet, 31, 89
First Symphony, 31, 32, 81
First Violin Sonata, 84, 97
Five Orchestral Songs (Berg), 66
Fourth Symphony, 31, 59, 67, 80–91, 89, 104, 108, 123
Fourth Violin Sonata, 120
"Funeral March for Chin-Chin" 17

The General Slocum, 58
"General William Booth's Entrance into Heaven," 66, 75–79
Goosens, Eugene, 89, 104
Griggs, John Cornelius, 26–27, 28, 35

Halloween, 58
Harrison, Lou, 44, 120, 121
Hawthorne, Nathaniel, 85
   "The Celestial Railroad," 85
"Hells Bells," 33, 34
Hindemith, Paul, 111, 113
"Holiday Quickstep," 17
Hyperion Theatre Orchestra, 28

"Ilmenau" (Goethe), 60
impressionism in Ives's music, 83
Ives & Myrick, 53–55, 103
Ives, Charles Edward,
   and World War I, 92–97
   as athlete, 17–18, 22, 25
   as organist, 19, 24, 27, 43, 43, 51–52
   as student, 38, 39, 53–55
   in insurance, 38, 39, 53–55
   last hours, 127

Ives, Edith, 62, 106
Ives, George, 3, 4, 5, 6, 26, 38
    as music teacher, 9, 10, 11, 12, 14
    as band leader, 5–6, 16
Ives, Joseph Moss ("Mossie"), 6–7, 10, 56

Kirkpatrick, John, 83, 117–119, 120, 123, 127

"Let There Be Light," 45

Mahler, Gustav, xii, xiii, 45, 48, 65, 83, 102
The Majority, 94–95
Memos, 11, 112–113
Milhaud, Darius, 104
Musical Courier review, 47
Mutual Life Insurance Company, 39, 40, 53
    the Raymond Agency, 40, 53
Myrick, Julian, 40, 53–55, 93

New England Holidays symphony, 33, 66–67, 79, 113, 120
    "Thanksgiving," 51
    "Washington's Birthday," 51, 89
    "Fourth of July," 58, 97
New Music, 108
New York Herald Tribune review, 118–119
New York Little Symphony Orchestra, 45
New York Times reviews, 46, 105, 115

114 Songs, xiii, 17, 75, 102
ostinato, 90

Pan-American concerts, 109–114
Parker, Horatio, 25, 27, 28–29, 30, 31, 32, 35, 47, 98
Pine Mountain, 56, 58
polytonality, 20, 50, 107

"Postface" to *114 Songs*, xiii
"Poverty Flat," 36, 42, 56
Prelude and Postlude for a Thanksgiving Service, 33, 49
Pro Musica, 104, 106
Pro Musica Quarterly, 104
Prunières, Henry, review, 113
"Psalm 67," 30, 45, 50, 120
"Psalm 90," 45
"Psalm 100," 45
"Psalm 150," 45
Pulitzer Prize, 45, 120–121
Puritan character in Ives's music, 33, 35, 49–50, 89

quarter tones, study of, 14–15, 107

Riegger, Wallingford, 107, 111
Robert Browning Overture, 79
Ruggles, Carl, 75, 107, 109, 111
    Men and Mountains, 109, 123, 127

Schmitz, E. Robert, 101, 103–104, 113
Schoenberg, Arnold, xiii, 48, 65, 66
    Gurrelieder, 83
    Pierrot Lunaire, 66
Schumann, Robert, 65
"Serenity" (Whittier), 125
Slonimsky, Nicolas, 80, 89, 108, 109, 123
"Slow March," 17
"A Song of Mory's," 33
"South Wind" (Heine), 60, 62
"Spring Song" (Heine), 60
Stravinsky, Igor, viii, 48, 51, 66, 111
    Petrushka, 51
    Rite of Spring, 51, 66
Szigeti, Joseph, 120

Talmadge, David, 102
"Theatre Orchestra Set," 28
"Three Harvest Home Chorales," 45
"They Are There," 95–96
Third Symphony, 44, 45, 59, 120–121
    "Old Folks Gathern'," 44
    "Children's Day," 44
    "Communion," 44
Thoreau, Henry David, 38, 56, 58, 68, 72–73, 91, 100
    Walden, 56, 58, 72–73, 91
Three Places in New England, 16, 66, 79, 108
Tone Roads, 79
Transcendentalism in Ives's music, 67–69, 71, 73–74, 80, 85, 90,
    115–116, 127
Twitchell, Dave, 25, 58, 59
Twain, Mark, 59–60, 62

Universe Symphony, 125–127

Variations on "America," 20, 49

"World's Highway," 60

"A Yale-Princeton Football Game," 28